Quest
for
Dion
Fortune

Quest
for
Dion
Fortune

JANINE CHAPMAN
FOREWORD by KENNETH GRANT

SAMUEL WEISER, INC.

York Beach, Maine

First published in 1993 by
Samuel Weiser, Inc.
Box 612
York Beach, Maine 03910

Library of Congress Cataloging-in-Publication Data

Chapman. Janine. 1944-
   Quest for Dion Fortune / by Janine Chapman
         p.   cm.
      1. Fortune, Dion.   2. Occultists--England--Biography.
   3. Fraternity of the Inner Light--Biography.   I. Title.
BF1408.2.F67C48   1993
133' .092--dc20
[B]   93-10006
                                                                                CIP

ISBN 0-87728-775-9

MG

The cover was created from a photograph of Glastonbury Tor taken by the author.

Typeset in 10 point Palatino

Printed in the United States of America
99 98 97 96 95 94 93
10 9 8 7 6 5 4 3 2 1

The paper used in this publication meets the minimum requirements of the American
National Standard for permanence of Paper for Printed Library Materials Z39.48-1984.

In Memory of
W. Ernest Butler
1898-1978

Contents

FOREWORD

"The word which shall come to save the world, shall be uttered by a woman. . . . Hers is the light of the heavens, and the brightest of the planets of the holy seven. She is the fourth dimension; the eyes which enlighten; the power which draweth inward to God. And her kingdom cometh; the day of the exaltation of woman. And her reign shall be greater than the reign of man." So prophesied Anna Kingsford, a celebrated mystic of the 19th century. The vision may be true, or it may not, and although woman and man are designated metaphors for intuition and ordinary cognition it has a curiously modern ring. Some such notion no doubt inspired Janine Chapman to set out on her quest for Dion Fortune. Like Anna Kingsford, Dion Fortune was at one time a member of the Theosophical Society founded by another visionary, Helena Blavatsky. Unlike Blavatsky, however, Fortune's life was not a series of tempestuous adventures crying out to be seized upon by numerous biographers, so Chapman set herself a harder task.

Like many occultists, Fortune discouraged the personality cult, and although she herself had an unusually strong personality, she did not allow it to color her technical writings. In her novels, however, we obtain frequent glimpses of a startlingly unorthodox and skillful occultist who succeeded in gaining access to other worlds, other dimensions, through an adaptation of Eastern techniques usually associated with Tantric yoga. This amalgam appeared to be at variance with the tilt of her frequently expressed preference for the Western Esoteric Tradition as epitomized in the Hermetic Order of the Golden Dawn, to which she also once belonged, and it created in her a dichotomy which becomes evident on comparing her instructional writings with her fiction. In Fortune's day certain opinions were considered acceptable only if expressed through the mouths of fictional characters. In her novels she was free to give rein to her inmost nature and they focus upon her the light of Kingsford's prophecy.

We recognize in Fortune a dedicated priestess, a priestess of Isis—as Blavatsky before her had been— of Isis unveiled and bearing her Secret Doctrine. Fortune, too, had her Cosmic Doctrine, concerned, as was Blavatsky's, with vast cycles of time, alien life-waves and superhuman entities. We realize, soon enough, that we are confronted not with the anomaly of a female priest—a notion as grotesque as that of a male priestess—but with a genuine vehicle of the mysteries of Old Isis, of the moon, the sea, the fertile and barren earth, and also of a New Isis whose radiant influence is emanating from dimensions beyond the range of our merely geocentric conceptions of the universe.

Yet aside from Fortune's far-flung flights to other worlds, in controlled trances warded by fellow initiates, she brought a special message for half our race. Speaking through her magical personality, Lilith Le Fay, she declares in one of her novels, "I came back to the world yet once again as the priestess of the Great Goddess bringing with me the memory of forgotten arts, one of which is the art of being a woman."

It is in this role that she inspires today so many who read her books and endeavor to put into practice the magical arts and skills that she taught. She was undoubtedly the first major Western occultist actually to demonstrate the role of woman as an active initiator into the Mysteries, rather than as a passive vehicle of transmission from elemental and trans-mundane forces. Prior to Fortune, no woman—including Blavatsky, Kingsford, Besant, and Bailey—had publicly and pointedly defined the mechanism of sexual polarity in the service of practical magic and sorcery. Such teaching was lacking in the Theosophical Society as in the Golden Dawn, the two chief sources of Arcane Knowledge in the Western hemisphere in recent times. Aleister Crowley alone was throwing light upon this area of occultism, which is still held to be as highly dangerous now as it was when Fortune was publishing her books in the 1920s and 1930s. She was, of course, aware of Crowley's knowledge of these matters and of their connection with Tantra.

She noted in *Moon Magic*, "The use of the actual woman as the goddess is high Tantric magic." It was one reason why she decided eventually to meet Crowley. I was fortunate in being present on one of these occasions, which occurred not many months before the deaths of both these great initiates. The allusion to two black cocks, mentioned by Janine Chapman, was occasioned by Fortune's need for precise information concerning a ritual that she intended to describe in a future novel. Chapman has researched Fortune's early involvement with poultry farming, but the information she sought was not on the agenda of instruction she was likely to have received on the farm! Their conversation turned also upon "Hidden Masters" and "Secret Chiefs," in connection—I think—with *The Cosmic Doctrine*. Fortune made the interesting observation that, like Crowley himself, she had been in contact with an Entity every bit as awesome as Aiwass who had provided Crowley with *The Book of the Law*. One can believe this after reading Fortune's novels.

That Crowley thought highly of Dion Fortune and her Fraternity of the Inner Light is suggested by the fact that he had already attempted to meet her, and that after her death he wrote a letter to a close associate in which he claimed that Fortune and he had "a very secret understanding"; he also expressed a desire to take over her organization. Fortune's initial reluctance to meet Crowley may have been due in part to the fact that she lampooned him in one of her stories, but her qualms were no doubt overridden by her essential inner accordance with the basic tenets of the New Aeon. She made this accordance clear in a letter that she wrote to Crowley in 1945 from which Janine Chapman quotes.

Another great occultist divined the essential Fortune. I lent one of her novels to Austin Osman Spare who returned it with a characteristically laconic comment, "She's one of us!" I feel sure that all who are able to tap the deeper Dion—and there is a growing number of "us"—experience a similar sense of communion with this extraordinary woman.

Kenneth Grant
Winter 1993
London

ACKNOWLEDGMENTS

I am grateful to all the people who helped me on my quest by sharing personal information and indicating avenues of research.

My greatest debt is to the late W. Ernest Butler, who gave me the confidence to continue my search and who shared vital secrets with me regarding Dion Fortune's life. I am grateful also to Kenneth Grant for his information on Dion Fortune's friendship with Aleister Crowley; to John Symonds for his information on the Fortune-Crowley correspondence; to Charles Fielding for clarification regarding the magical polarity experiments; to William Breeze of the Ordo Templi Orientis; to the late Israel Regardie for recounting his meetings with Dion Fortune and Penry Evans; to Christopher Hyatt for permission to reprint Israel Regardie's letter; to Elizabeth Hess, the last Principal of Studley College, who pointed me to the University of Reading Library; to the anonymous archivist at the University of Reading who prepared the report about Violet Firth's stay at Studley College; to Trevor Bottomley of the University of Reading for permission to reprint the report; and to W. F. Ryan of the Warburg Institute for providing me with a copy of the letter from Dion Fortune to Aleister Crowley.

I am thankful to Helah Fox for her memories of Dion and the Inner Light Fraternity; to the late Evelyn Heathfield for her memories of Violet Firth at Studley College; to Mr. and Mrs. Heathfield of Lewes, Sussex, for their gracious hospitality; to Hope Todd for her psychic hook-up with Dion Fortune; to the proprietress of the guest house where I stayed in Southampton; and to the late John Shelly for entertaining me at Chalice Orchard.

My thanks also go to Peter Valentine of Brightenterprize in Cambridge, Massachusetts, proprietor of The Aquarian Age Bookstore, to Nancy Varner of the Boston Public Library, to

Leonard Schweitzer of The Glastonbury Bookshop in Tallahassee, Florida; to Charles Fielding, Carr Collins, and Alan Richardson for their two comprehensive biographies of Dion Fortune, and to the Society of the Inner Light for permission to quote small passages from Dion Fortune's books.

Finally, I wish to thank my friend Rosemary Dudley for keeping my research materials safe for fifteen years, my friend Canary Knight for his advice and encouragement, my aunt Isabel Devine for teaching me the skills of scholarship, my mother Florence Chapman, and my sons, Colin and Liam, for their love and support.

Introduction

"Do what thou wilt shall be the whole of the Law!"To the surly rhythm of the Crowley cult, Dion Fortune's "sane occultism" plays a tempered counterpoint. These two great occultists represented opposite paths. But their separate strains reflect more than two eccentric personalities. They reveal the distinct fashion in which two adepts performed the Great Work.

They were contemporaries; Dion Fortune, nee Violet Firth, was born in 1891, Crowley in 1875. They died within a year of each other—1946 and 1947 respectively. Both were nursed on Kabbalah and initiated in the Golden Dawn. Both sought the long-buried wine of the old gods: ancient, pure, and powerful; both called Britain home; both sought personal and racial identity in the holy places of their native land.

But while Crowley's behavior made him an outcast, Dion Fortune succeeded in integrating her magical personality with her everyday obligations and goals, and she was sensitive to the time and place within which she lived. Dion Fortune never lost the ability to function and serve in ordinary society. In fact she went far beyond this simple achievement. She founded a stable occult fraternity that exists to this day. She was a beneficial influence on many people who came within her sphere. She was remembered by her students reverently as a "guide, philosopher, and friend."

In the past, many of the people who thought of themselves as magicians were extraordinary personalities, marked by a mysterious sensitivity to supernatural forces and influences. Some were spiritually sincere, dedicated to the worship of their gods and to the teaching of their knowledge. But frequently the intensity of their visions caused violent fluctuations between mania and depression. Some had emotional and interpersonal problems. Some were arrogant, cruel, selfish, and petty. For some, their efforts at helping others were inappropriate, even destructive. For others, their attempts to communicate their experiences were confused or undecipherable.

Dion Fortune understood these problems and made it her business to address them. Besides writing books on various aspects of occultism, and several fine occult novels, she wrote articles for *The Occult Review*, edited her own journal, *The Inner Light* magazine, and lectured publicly on occult topics.

But it is not only Dion's teachings that are valuable to us today. Information about her personality and character traits are just as important. Sexually, she was modest, faithful, and chaste. Her marriage lasted almost twelve years. She had several deep, long-term friendships. As a woman, she set an example of super-achievement, self-sacrifice, and personal integrity. She had excellent management skills and organizational ability, and she exemplified a high standard of professional and ethical behavior. Perhaps most important of all, she had a talent for inspiring and bringing out the best in others.

After all, the real "work" of a magician is to know and master his or her own self. This fact makes the study of this type of person different from that of a poet or artist to whose work biographical information can legitimately be considered irrelevant. The magician's task is to concentrate and manipulate the diverse forces in his or her own nature until those forces interact, disintegrate, and change to emerge reassembled and reborn. What occurs is not only a mystical experience or immediate perception of the presence of an almighty and supreme power, it is a complex rebuilding of the machinery of experience and perception itself.

Violet's transformation from a shy, vulnerable adolescent into the strong, magnetic leader that she became is of vital interest to those of us who stumble along the path of spiritual development. It was this desire to know Dion Fortune as a person that motivated me many years ago to seek out more information about her life than was currently available. This concern became very important to me. You could even say it became an obsession. It eventually led me on an adventurous journey across the Atlantic Ocean to

England, Dion Fortune's birthplace and lifelong home. There I met associates of hers who enlightened me about many aspects of her life and character.

In my quest for information about Dion Fortune, however, I encountered two major obstacles. First, Dion's writings are largely lacking in personal reference. Taking the classic stance of the adept, she obscured the details of her life and the true nature of her personality behind a cloak of glamour and illusion. Although she later opposed those who made a fetish of secrecy, she was cautious in her method of instruction and maintained the traditional reticence in everything she wrote for publication. When I began my quest, I had to guess at the facts of Dion's inner and outer life by studying her novels. In these romantic, magical tales she used parts of herself and people she knew to create the fictional characters. The only time she spoke openly about herself was when she told the story of the mysterious psychic attack that caused her to pursue the study of psychology and occultism. But even then she was intentionally vague and elusive, naming neither people nor places.

The second obstacle to my research efforts was the Fraternity of the Inner Life itself, now called the Society of the Inner Light. The core of the society has always operated as a mystery group. Information about its inner workings are kept in absolute secrecy. Information about Dion Fortune, except that which has been published in her books, is also kept secret. If Dion left any diaries or letters, only the inner group of the Society of the Inner Light knows.

W. E. Butler, author of *The Magician: His Training and Work*, was a student of Dion Fortune's from 1925 until her death and an Inner Light member from 1925 until his death in 1978. He believed that after she passed away, the leading members of the Society disposed of Dion's personal papers and effects.[1] In a conversation with me in 1974, he referred to the matter as "the incinerator business." Whether this event actually occurred, we will probably never know. Mr. Butler admitted he was not present at the time, and the

---

[1] Kenneth Grant also told me that he believed the Society did destroy her papers.

Inner Light has refused to comment. When I met Mr. Butler in January of 1974, he showed me a Celtic cross he said Dion had used on the altar at Chalice Orchard in Glastonbury. He said he had rescued this cross from the fire, referring to the disposal of her personal papers and possessions. To this day, the Society of the Inner Light declines to communicate with outsiders on the subject of Dion Fortune.

In spite of the difficulties facing anyone researching her life, however, two fine biographies have been produced: *The Story of Dion Fortune* by Charles Fielding and Carr Collins, and *Priestess* by Alan Richardson. *The Story of Dion Fortune* is very informative, particularly regarding the Dr. Moriarty period, life at Chalice Orchard, and the history and inner workings of the Inner Light Fraternity. This book lacks footnotes, but Mr. Fielding has assured me that his sources of information are valid and that they originate from older members of the Society of the Inner Light. *Priestess* is a sensitive work and carefully researched; Richardson's primary source being Christine Hartley, one of Dion Fortune's students.

Quest for Dion Fortune is not another biography. It details my personal odyssey in 1973 and 1974 to obtain information about Dion Fortune's life. This book is the fruit of my study, travel, conversation, and meditation, and supplies previously unpublished and generally unknown facts about her life. Most of the people who knew Dion Fortune had died before Fielding or Richardson began their research, which caused significant gaps in their accounts. After reading these two books, certain mysteries remain unsolved; important questions remain unanswered. I was fortunate to meet several important contacts while they were still living. For this reason, I feel I have something of value to add to her story.

Included is correspondence of mine with Israel Regardie, Kenneth Grant, Christine Hartley, Iona Cammell, and others. I have included transcriptions of tapes made for me by W. Ernest Butler and a tape of my personal meeting with him at his home in Southampton, England, on January 9, 1974. Butler is well-known as author of *The Magician, His Training and Work; Apprenticed to Magic; Magic and the Western Tradition;* and several other books, most of which are still in print. He was a member of the Fraternity of the Inner Light from 1925.

Of particular note is the fact that I had the good fortune to discover the identity of the "educational establishment" where Violet Firth suffered the psychic attack she wrote about in *Psychic Self-Defense*, as well as the identity of the infamous warden of the school. Dion never names the establishment at which this event took place and never gives the whole story, most likely because of her reluctance to sully the reputation of the school. But the school has been closed since August 1969. The warden is dead and buried as are most, if not all, of the persons involved in this story. I feel that those interested have waited long enough and it is finally time to tell the truth.

BOOKS BY DION FORTUNE

Magic and Esoteric Study
Applied Magic
Aspects of Occultism
The Cosmic Doctrine
Esoteric Orders and their Work
Esoteric Philosophy of Love and Marriage
Glastonbury: Avalon of the Heart
Practical Occultism in Daily Life
Psychic Self-Defense
Sane Occultism
Spiritualism in the Light of Occult Science
Through the Gates of Death
The Training and Work of an Initiate

Mysticism
Mystical Meditations on the Collects
Mystical Qabalah

Fiction
The Demon Lover
The Goat Foot God
Moon Magic
The Sea Priestess
Secrets of Dr. Taverner
The Winged Bull

Psychology (by Violet M. Firth)
The Machinery of the Mind
The Problem of Purity
Psychology of the Servant Problem

Quest
for
Dion
Fortune

Chapter 1

THE QUEST
FOR DION FORTUNE BEGINS

I first heard of Dion Fortune in 1969. I was living in Cambridge, Massachusetts at the time. I had just completed a correspondence course in astrology and was beginning to branch out in search of more information about the occult. Since childhood I had been fascinated by this mysterious field of knowledge, which was excluded from the curriculum of every college and university. I possessed a few books along these lines that I had purchased at the impressionable age of 15 at a sale of occult books at Brentano's Bookstore on Fifth Avenue in New York City. Among the books I bought were Montague Summers' *The Vampire, His Kith and Kin, The Werewolf*, and *The Geography of Witchcraft*, and the three volume *Materials Toward the History of Witchcraft* collected by Henry Charles Lea and George L. Burr. These books fascinated me with their wealth of scholarly detail on these weird and fantastic subjects.

Many years later, when I moved to Cambridge with my husband and 3-year-old son, the United States was in the midst of the hippie era and Harvard Square was one of its vital centers. The saffron-robed Hare Krishnas chanted in the street. Scientology representatives hung out looking for "raw meat" (the facetious term they applied to potential recruits). Members of The Process Church of the Final Judgment strode through the square dressed in black from head to toe. Long-haired boys and girls in bell-bottomed jeans, Indian shirts, and funky jewelry wandered through the Cambridge Common where the smell of marijuana was frequently in the air.

There were two occult bookstores in Cambridge at the time—The Sphinx, which was then located on lower Massachusetts Avenue opposite Harvard Yard, and The Aquarian Age, located first on Cambridge Street and later conveniently on a side street in the heart of Harvard Square. I visited both bookstores often but liked The Aquarian Age best because of the distinctive way it was designed and the special atmosphere it generated.

This store had a brick doorway with a painted bricked-in arch above it that looked like a crown. There was a mirror on the entrance door so the first thing you saw was yourself. Above the entrance was painted in white, happy, wavy lettering on a dark purple background, "The Aquarian Age, Books & Objects."

The interior walls were painted a dark purple sprinkled with specks of gold and silver. The books were arranged in floor to ceiling shelves painted a golden mustard. There was a table in the center of the store draped with a dark velvet cloth and covered with books. To the left of the entrance was a display case with a glass top outlined with ivory colored fur. This case was covered with pamphlets on subjects such as crystal gazing and palmistry, with decks of tarot cards and various occult curios. Behind the display case stood the owner, Peter Valentine, a handsome, dark-haired, mysterious young man who intrigued me. He also owned and operated Moon River Tearoom on Charles Street in Boston and was the creator of The Dial, a fortune-telling device mounted on a leather band and worn on the wrist like a watch.

Opposite the entrance, in the corner, was a big comfortable brown chair beside which was a floor lamp covered with yellow papier-mâché. It was a happy, gentle place and it was here that I first opened a book by the woman known as Dion Fortune.

It was *The Mystical Qabalah* that I read first. It was a hardcover edition that cost a significant amount of the weekly salary earned from typing payroll checks in the comptroller's office at Harvard University's Holyoke Center. In fact, to escape the boring routine of my job, I often visited The Aquarian Age Bookstore on my lunch hour, always coming out feeling uplifted. For the rest of the afternoon I would look forward to the coming evening when I could go home and travel in my mind to Chalice Orchard, 3 Queensborough Terrace, and the other haunts of that great female occultist. Eventually I read all of her books. Her novels were a wonderful experience. I looked forward to each one and read them rapidly with total absorption. Her books became a significant part of my growing personal library of works on occult and magical subjects.

At that time I was a student of Ophiel (aka Edward Peach) through his correspondence course in The Foundations of Occult Knowledge offered by The Gnostic Institute in St. Paul, Minnesota.

I was busy learning about the Inner Planes, doing practical work with occult symbols, keeping a magical diary, working the Qabalistic Cross Ritual, and beginning experiments in astral projection. I also did horoscopes for people and gave tarot readings in my home.

My first husband, J. Michael James, and I were involved in founding a company called Cyborg Corporation, which manufactured some of the earliest biofeedback equipment, including "alpha machines" for recording and controlling human brain waves. When Michael started drawing a salary from the company, I was able to quit my job and devote myself to taking care of our son and pursue my occult studies in earnest.

By this time I had read most of Dion Fortune's work and had begun to look for more material about her personally. I couldn't find anything. I had been looking for a task to do, something concrete other than studying and doing rituals. I decided to undertake researching the life of Dion Fortune with the hope of eventually writing her biography.

Our Dion Fortune was really Violet Mary Firth, who was born on December 6, 1890 under the sign of Sagittarius, the Archer, at Bryn-y-Bia in the town of Llandudno in Wales. She was not an orphan as some people thought. She was a member of the Firth family of Sheffield, a city in the north of England in south Yorkshire county. The family was widely-known for the manufacture of stainless steel. Her father, Arthur Firth, ran a hotel in the town called the Craigside Hydropathic Establishment. In 1906, the Firths moved to London where Violet and her mother came under the spell of the newly founded Christian Science Church. The basic tenet of that faith, that "all is Mind," and its converse "matter does not exist," undoubtedly influenced her during the impressionable adolescent years.

Although Christian Science did much to awaken Violet's interest in spiritual matters, it was a crisis in her twentieth year that really "rent the veil." The principal at an agricultural training college where Violet was employed, managed in a series of interviews to destroy most of the girl's self-confidence and personality structure by techniques of mental manipulation which she had learned in India. It is this experience which Violet later related in her book *Psychic Self-Defense*: "My attention was first turned to psychology, and subsequently to occultism as the real key to psychology, by the personal experience of a psychic attack which left me with shattered health for a considerable period."[1]

In *The Story of Dion Fortune*, Charles Fielding says that the place where this attack occurred, and that Dion refers to merely as an "educational establishment" or "training college," was a "residential commercial school" in Weston-super-Mare. However, he does not support his theory with any evidence. Everything he says about the incident is taken from Dion's own description in *Psychic Self-Defense*.

Alan Richardson also relies on *Psychic Self-Defense*. He says that the place could have been either St. George's Secretarial College in London or the British Colonial Training Institute near the town of Thursley in Surrey, but he admits that he is merely speculating. In fact, it was none of these places; it was Studley Agricultural College in Warwickshire, and the years were 1911-1913.

I had the privilege of learning this information from several primary sources. First of all, in January of 1974, I met Mrs. Evelyn Heathfield, who had been with Violet Firth at Studley College. A transcript of my tape-recorded interview with her is printed later on in this book. In addition, another former classmate of Violet's at Studley, Mrs. Alice King, sent me her impressions of Violet. Finally, the last principal of Studley, Miss Elizabeth Hess, referred me to the archivist at the University of Reading, where the school records were deposited in 1969 when Studley was closed. The archivist confirmed Violet's attendance, and it was his report that revealed the facts of her tenure there.

W. E. Butler felt strongly that the place where Violet Firth experienced her psychic attack was Studley College. Although he never advanced his opinion in writing, a key to the mystery occurs at the end of chapter 6 of his book, *Apprenticed to Magic*. He refers to Dion Fortune mentioning this school to him. He calls it a "magical school," which it was not. But he adds that "each

---

[1] Dion Fortune, *Psychic Self-Defense* (York Beach, ME: Samuel Weiser, 1992), p.9.

student had a small patch of garden," and then, "it was . . . held that the principal could observe clairvoyantly the inner feelings of the students."

Studley was, in fact, a horticultural training school, and many of the students did have their own small garden. Furthermore, the warden of Studley during Violet's time there was thought by many of the students to have the same clairvoyant ability mentioned by Mr. Butler. My sources of information regarding Studley College also told me much about the infamous warden, whose name I learned was Dr. Lillias Hamilton. Mrs. Evelyn Heathfield recounted her memories of Dr. Hamilton to me. Miss Katharine Evans, sister of Miriam Evans, a classmate of Violet's at Studley, commented on Dr. Hamilton in a letter to me. She also sent me copies of the *News About the Guild*, an "in-house" newsletter published by the warden for the years during which Violet attended. This newsletter proved to be an invaluable source of information.

The experience at Studley caused a radical change in the young Violet. It affected her reasoning ability and weakened her physically and emotionally for many years afterward. The experience did, however, serve to kindle her curiosity about the powers of the mind, a curiosity that eventually led her to the study of psychology and occultism.

Violet studied psychology and psychoanalysis at the University of London. Her own writings reveal the influence of Freud and Adler. It may not have been until later in life that she began to read Jung.[2] Also early in her studies she became interested in the writings of Francis Aveling, whose books *Personality and Will* and *Directing Mental Energy* deal with the subject of human motivation and values. Perhaps the energy with which Dion Fortune was to pursue her many interests was harnessed through an application of Aveling's ideas.

Her life reveals a compulsion to direct her diverse energies, realizing their function as raw materials for the making of her personality. This compulsion took the form of a quest for the source of

---

[2] The author was told this by Helah Fox in the interview transcribed in chapter 5.

"Power," but her desire for real, applicable techniques saved her from self-delusion. In a time when the borderland between psychology and occultism was a forest of brambles, she perceived the possibility that the way out lay through the field of psychophysiology.[3] Only her obvious erudition in occult subjects prevented the scorn she would otherwise have received from the majority of her occult contemporaries for this unorthodox suggestion. In the last ten years of her life, she stressed repeatedly that not enough was known to justify definite statements about these matters, leading the way for a less dogmatic occultism unfettered by the fear of science.

Psychoanalysis was enjoying the height of fashionable popularity when Violet Firth became a lay psychoanalyst at a clinic in London. (Alan Richardson feels this was a clinic associated with the London Royal Free Hospital, which in turn was closely affiliated with the psychology department of the University of London. Christine Hartley says that Violet Firth worked at the Tavistock Clinic.)[4] At the same time, many people were demanding the requirement of a medical degree for the practice of psychoanalysis in an effort to secure respect for it as a science and to free it from the tinge of occultism.

While still working at this clinic, Violet came in contact with the Theosophical Society. The society was located nearby and offered meals to respectable outsiders along with lectures and information about Theosophy. Violet attended a meditation class and used the society's library in Tavistock Square. A book called *The Ancient Wisdom* stimulated her receptive mind to a series of visionary meetings with the masters of occult philosophy.

Shortly after, however, the First World War broke out and Violet joined the Land Army. The Food Production Department of the Ministry of Agriculture supervised the various women's agricultural committees forming in each county and selected volunteers. Violet applied and was accepted. Undoubtedly, her

---

[3] For more information about Dion's thoughts on psychophysiology consult her books *Sane Occultism* and *Machinery of the Mind*. See especially chapter I, "The Physical Vehicle of Consciousness" in *Machinery of the Mind*.

[4] Miss Hartley stated in a letter to the author dated March 22, 1974, that "I did know Violet Firth when she had just begun work at the Tavistock Clinic."

experience at Studley Agricultural College was an important factor in her admission to the program. Alan Richardson's assumption in *Priestess* that Violet had nothing in her background to prepare her for the difficulty of this work was innocently in error. In fact, Violet was very well prepared due to her training and experience at Studley College. Further, her work during her government service at a laboratory belonging to the food production department continued her scientific training begun at Studley, training she would continue to make use of when she returned to her psychological and occult studies. While at this laboratory, she discovered a means of making milk from soybeans and described this process in her little-known book, *The Soya Bean*, long out of print. Richardson's comment that this discovery could have made her rich was accurate. Others were later to capitalize on this same process.

Among the diverse varieties of psychoanalytic techniques practiced at that time were the most interesting methods of a certain Theodore Moriarty, fictionalized later by Dion Fortune in *The Secrets of Dr. Taverner*. (Dr. Taverner was *not* modeled on the Scottish occultist, Dr. John Brodie-Innes, as some have speculated.) Behind the facade of the Science Arts and Crafts Society, he taught occult doctrine and became involved in cases of vampirism, psychic attack, and other unusual examples of abnormal psychology. After the war, Violet was drawn to the little group of Dr. Moriarty's disciples. A Freemason and a man of intense personal magnetism, Moriarty's influence on Violet was more than an intellectual stimulation; he awakened her emotional and spiritual potential, as well.

In 1919, Violet joined a branch of the Alpha et Omega (A.O.), one of two daughter lodges of the Golden Dawn Amen-Ra Temple in Edinburgh headed by Brodie-Innes. Both of these daughter lodges were located in London. One of the branches was led by a woman named Maiya Tranchell-Hayes. Mrs. Tranchell-Hayes had acquired an extensive knowledge of occult and psychological subjects and was skilled in the practice of ritual magic. In addition, she had had first-hand experience in the study of mental pathology while she was living with her psychiatrist husband at a large residential psychiatric facility, which he ran. Mrs. Hayes perceived Dion's potential and taught and trained her in many phases of magical work.

The other daughter lodge was under the direction of Moina Mathers. It was during this period, for her initiation into one of these Golden Dawn Lodges, that Violet took the magical name *Deus Non Fortuna*, of which Dion Fortune is a shortened form.

In 1924, simultaneously with her Golden Dawn activities, Violet believed herself to have received instruction from the Inner Planes to renew her contact with the Theosophical Society. She did and eventually became president of the Christian Mystic Lodge section of the society, which was dedicated to the Master Jesus. By 1927, however, serious differences had arisen between Dion Fortune and the other members of the Theosophical Society and she resigned.

At the same time, Dion was advancing rapidly in the Golden Dawn, but she had become impatient with the atmosphere of the London Temple, which she claimed was too inbred and lacking in vitality. Her idea was to form another group as an "outer court" to the Golden Dawn to draw in new people. Mrs. Mathers agreed to this idea, and in 1922 the Fraternity of the Inner Light was born. Some of the Inner Light's early members were Dion's former pupils from the Christian Mystic Lodge of the Theosophical Society who had resigned at the same time she did. In 1925, she began to publish frequently in the *Occult Review* and advertisements for the meetings and correspondence courses of the fraternity soon began to appear.

Moina Mathers became envious of Dion Fortune's new status in the occult community, and she tried to expel Dion from the Golden Dawn. Ostensibly, her reason was the publicity the order's teachings were receiving at Dion's hands. Moina claimed that Dion's book, *The Esoteric Philosophy of Love and Marriage*, contained some of the inner secrets of the order. When this attack was parried (Dion had not attained the grade necessary for acquiring these "secrets"), Mrs. Mathers claimed that certain symbols were not appearing in Dion Fortune's aura and expelled her on that account. Needless to say, the Inner Light continued as before. There was a center at Glastonbury and at 3 Queensborough Terrace in London. The inner group, i.e., those people who lived with Dion Fortune permanently, spent all their time on occult work—trances, personal regeneration, meditation, and study. Other members held regular jobs during the day and lived at 3 Queensborough Terrace, participating in meetings and rituals in the evening.

Dion Fortune married a physician, a Welshman named Thomas Penry Evans. Evans was born under the Air sign Libra on September 27, 1892 at Farmer's Field, Pontardulais, an industrial town in the south of Wales. His father was a shearer in the local tin works. The family later moved to Llanelli, another town in South Wales.

Evans received his M.D. in 1924 and practiced in Llanelli for a year. Then he took a position as House Surgeon and Medical Registrar for Charing Cross Hospital where he gave his address as 3 Queensborough Terrace, the headquarters for the Fraternity of the Inner Light. Penry's sister Hazel, then a student nurse, also lived at 3 QT. She performed the services of a maid, her pay there helping her to finish school.

Nobody seems to know exactly where or how Penry and Dion met. It would have had to be before he took up residence at 3 QT in 1925. Possibly they met when she was taking courses at the University of London. He was undoubtedly attracted by her mystical aura and exotic interests as well as by her keen intelligence and questing mind. It is easy to imagine the two of them having long, stimulating conversations on subjects such as psychology, psychophysiology, and the occult. This intellectual element in their relationship may very well have been stronger than their mutual sexual attraction, which may not have been very strong, except possibly at first.

Although Dion was born in Wales, as was he, her family came from Sheffield in the Yorkshire county of England. Physically, she was of the large-framed, pale skinned Aryan/Nordic/Celtic stock whereas Penry was a typical small dark Welshman most likely largely of Iberian blood. Penry's social background was working class whereas hers was upper middle class.

Symbolically and emotionally Penry stimulated Dion's Welsh contact, which she could claim by virtue of the location of her birth. He undoubtedly stirred up the dark underside of her outgoing, gregarious nature. Romantically and magically, he probably served for her as a link with Mediterranean and Egyptian god-forms. For some time he was certainly the priest of her magical workings. As a doctor, or "medicine man" he had, in her eyes, much magical power and that power undoubtedly attracted her to him on all the "planes" of occult doctrine. Weaving him also into her romantic Arthurian notions, she called him Merl, after Merlin, the prophet and magician of Arthurian legend.

Violet and Penry were married on April 7, 1927 at Paddington Register Office when she was 36 and he 35. They took their honeymoon at Chalice Orchard in Glastonbury, Somerset where they were photographed together. This marriage photograph has turned out to be the only known photograph of Dion Fortune.

Fortune's contact with the world of medicine probably came through her husband, who exposed her to information she might not otherwise have acquired, and it undoubtedly had its effect on her approach to occultism. Over the period 1925-1935, when she was writing for the *Occult Review*, Dion's interpretations of occult phenomena appear more and more in psychophysiological rather than psychological terms. She hypothesized a relationship between the "chakras" of occult philosophy's "etheric body" and the endocrine glands with their secretions of hormones in the human organism. She knew also that the endocrine system was controlled in the brain. She may have been aware of the early experimental studies of the brain and the recording of brain waves, the early experimental studies of the emotions, and the correlation of electrical activity of the human brain and human emotions, studies that were being conducted for the most part in the United States. She would have heard of these studies through her husband and/or through reports of such research in British and American medical journals. Her conclusions on these subjects were anything but final. She realized that not enough was known to form anything but tentative theories and she said so honestly.

Because of the semipublic nature of the Fraternity of the Inner Light, people with potential aptitude for occult and magical work were encouraged to apply for membership. W. E. Butler, drawn by an article in the *Occult Review*, received his magical training in the fraternity. Under Dion's guidance, Mr. Butler became a magician in his own right. He authored several books, still popular today, including *Apprenticed to Magic* and *The Magician, His Training and Work*. As an old man, Mr. Butler would reaffirm his debt to Dion Fortune. He felt strongly about her beneficial influence, going so far as to say that whatever good there was in his character was due to Dion Fortune and to his other teacher, Robert King. In spite of the many changes the group went through after Dion Fortune's death, he remained a member.

Part of Dion Fortune's basic attitude was a willingness to relinquish previously held opinions if she later found them to be untrue. This attitude was carried over into her fraternity. In 1934 she was able to say that "the Fraternity of the Inner Light has undergone a rigorous and systematic process of . . . debunking, and rests upon what we believe to be a sound basis of psychological technique, scholarly tradition, and practical occultism."

With all due respect to the post-Dion Fortune Inner Light, it is my personal opinion that unfortunately this healthy philosophical outlook was to die with Dion Fortune herself. I do not feel she found a competent successor for her work. It wasn't that there weren't members who could actively assume administrative responsibility, there simply wasn't anyone of her caliber or her grade who could carry on with the level of magical working she had attained. This situation is not unusual in organizations where the leader and founder is a charismatic personality of exceptional abilities and achievement.

Dion Fortune felt a strong identity with what she called The Western Mystery Tradition. The location of her center at Chalice Orchard in Glastonbury reflects this perfectly. Layer upon layer of spiritual associations exist in Glastonbury: pagan, Christian, romantic. In addition, it seems that from the earliest days, Glastonbury has been associated with the cult of what is variously known as The Mother Goddess, Mary, and The Feminine Principle. When we realize that Dion herself was interested in this particular aspect of higher consciousness, and take into consideration her extreme sensitivity to atmospheres, the symbols associated with Glastonbury and her own personal symbols seem to blend.

In her prime, Dion was a strong, magnetic personality, physically imposing, of Viking build, and possessing the mysterious electric aura of the professional occultist. As Bernard Bromage put it in his article about her in the 1960 spring issue of the Spiritualist journal *Light*: "There was an odd atmosphere about her of the sibyl, the prophetess, the diver into deep occult seas." She had an active, intellectually curious mind that speculated constantly on many subjects. In addition, she became a thoroughly experienced and accomplished practitioner in the art of ritual magic. Besides teaching, lecturing, writing, designing, and producing rituals, Dion also spent much of her time in active psychotherapy with her Inner Light students. Of course, she had been trained for this work, but beyond her educational credentials she also possessed the potent

Fraternity ^{of}_{the} Inner Light

3, Queensborough Terrace

London, W.2

Warden:
DION FORTUNE

Christmas Recess

The last Meeting before the Xmas Recess will be on Monday, Dec. 19th, at 8.15 p.m., when an informal discussion will be held.
The Spring Term will open on Monday, January 16th, and the syllabus of lectures will be sent post free on application after January 1st, 1933.

Correspondence Courses

A series of Correspondence Courses has been worked out for the benefit of those who wish to make a serious study of occultism, but who are not in the position to attend lectures and classes in London.

The courses give a thorough grounding in Esoteric Science and are capable of taking the student a considerable distance.

The syllabus and conditions of enrolment may be had from 3, Queensborough Terrace, W.2, and it should be noted that the genuine courses are only to be obtained from this address, no other person or organizations being authorized to give them.

Figure 1. A sample page from the Occult Review, *December 1932.*

aura of the spiritual healer, so much so that her personality itself had a curative power on her students and on the society as a whole.

After the Second World War, Dion became involved in the popular cult of Spiritualism and in the investigations of the Society for Psychic Research. As usual, she retained her scientific yardstick, her probing for objective, empirical explanations for "supernatural" events.

In 1946, Dion Fortune died in London of blood poisoning from a badly extracted tooth. She had also been previously diagnosed as having leukemia. She was buried in Glastonbury Cemetery. The Inner Light continued on its own momentum, although it soon was no longer a magical fraternity. Certain members had criticized her openly while she was alive, due partially to fears of a "personality cult." So, after her death, these members instituted a policy of not encouraging interest on the part of anyone in the details of Dion's personal life.[5]

Other members left when they saw the changes that were occurring. It was Mr. Butler's opinion that the essential dynamism of the group evaporated entirely.

Eventually, two new magical groups were formed. One of these, Servants of the Light, was associated with Basil Wilby (aka Gareth Knight) of Helios Book Service in Glastonbury and with W. E. Butler. The other, Star & Cross, still has centers in London and in Dallas, Texas. Associated with the latter group are Charles Fielding and Carr Collins, authors of the first biography of Dion Fortune, *The Story of Dion Fortune*.

The original Inner Light, now calling itself the Society of the Inner Light, still exists. As of 1975, Ithell Colquhoun, author of *The Sword of Wisdom*, a history of the Golden Dawn and its affiliated movements, says that gradually the Christian aspect of the society dominated the Kabbalistic, hermetic, and orphic aspects, which were eventually dropped entirely. This may be largely true. However, in 1971, when I wrote to the Inner Light at its new headquarters at 39 Steele's Road, inquiring about their correspondence course, the materials I received stated that the course was based on two of Dion Fortune's books: *The Mystical Qabalah* and *The Cosmic*

---

[5] The author received this information from an early inner member of the Society of the Inner Light.

Doctrine. This would seem to indicate that the Kabbalistic aspect had not been totally ejected. *The Mystical Qabalah* is considered Dion Fortune's masterpiece. *The Cosmic Doctrine* is supposed to be a re-written version of *The Seven Aphorisms of Creation*, which are compilations of notes taken at Dr. Moriarty's lectures and which are the real "secrets of Dr. Taverner," the fictitious name Dion gave to Moriarty when she wrote her book, *The Secrets of Dr. Taverner.*

As in Dion Fortune's day, the Inner Group of the Society of the Inner Light and the Outer Group are separate entities. The Inner Group holds the central authority and decides matters of policy. Secrecy is a prime tenet of the Inner Group's code. This secrecy covers all information they possess regarding Dion Fortune, including any letters, diaries, notes, etc., which she may have left behind. Consequently, they will not correspond with outsiders on the subject of their founder.

Francis King, says in *Ritual Magic in England*, published in 1970, (in chapter 18, "Dion Fortune and the Fraternity of the Inner Light"), that in the 1950s and 1960s the Inner Light became involved in "practices alien to the Western Tradition derived from the more eccentric fringes of occultism and of physical and psychological therapy," including the writings of Alice A. Bailey and L. Ron Hubbard's Scientology. He said that the Inner Light was no longer a magical fraternity but was rather, as he put it, "a heterodox semi-Christian cult."[6]

• • •

After preliminary research into Dion Fortune's life, the historical background of the period—particularly the new psychologies that were popular then—I decided to contact people who had known her. The first person I wrote to was W. E. Butler, who had once been a student of hers. I wrote to him in October of 1972, in care of his publisher. Weeks and then months passed and I received no answer. Disappointed, I drew the conclusion that Mr. Butler thought me not worth answering. It was a shock months later to receive a letter from England with Mr. Butler's name and address on the flap.

---

[6] Francis King, *Ritual Magic in England* (Saffron Walden, England: Neville Spearman, 1970), p.158.

Mr. Butler explained that he had been ill, hence the delay in answering. He said he would be writing to me more fully in a few days and that whatever information he had concerning Dion Fortune he would gladly make available to me. I had suggested the spring or summer of 1974 as a possible date to meet him, but he was afraid he might not live that long, and promised to record something on a couple of cassette tapes and send them to me. He said he deeply appreciated my interest in Dion Fortune, and he would help me in whatever way he could.

I was elated by his response and by his words of encouragement, but his statement about his health alarmed me. I sent a reply dated February 27 in which I suggested flying immediately to England. He wrote back stating that it was not necessary to come so soon and suggested that we first try the tapes. He told me also that I would receive no assistance from the Society of the Inner Light. He did say that he knew someone who had been a fellow pupil of Dion Fortune at an agricultural college and that there were one or two ex-members of the Society of the Inner Light scattered about who knew her in the late thirties.

After reading the letter, I sat down to write a reply. I reproduce my letter here in full and the following letters by me to him because our long-distance written conversation highlights important information from Dion Fortune's life and literary labors. The correspondence also shows something of the urgency of my quest.

March 9, 1973

Dear Mr. Butler,

I have received your letter of March 3rd. It seems as if the best idea is for you to send me the tapes and for me to send you back my questions, etc. and for me not to come to England for several months. I would really rather do it this way but you had alarmed me in your first letter when you spoke of your health and I thought I should come right away. Then, when I didn't get a reply to my last two letters I got worried. I tried to reach you by phone but there was no listing in your name. Then I thought there might be someone at Helios Book Service who would know you and who could tell me how you were. I called and spoke to a man whose name I did not get who told me you were well and that he would mention to you that I was trying to reach you. I hope you will not be too annoyed that I did this. I will see the other people who knew Dion Fortune, but you are a very special link and I do not want it to break.

The rates will be low again starting in September. If you can tell me, meanwhile, as much as you can about the Dion Fortune you knew, my meeting with you will then be more meaningful.

I know about the Society of the Inner Light. Also, I have been puzzled about that remark in C. Wilson's book since I first read it, as the man described in *Psychic Self-Defense* which Wilson is referring to did not seem very much like Crowley at all. I would like to know who he really was. She says he was the head of "an occult college which was hidden away in the sandy fastnesses of the Hampshire barrens," (p. 43) and that she received her first training from him. Her descriptions of him (pp. 50-51) resemble closely her descriptions of "Dr. Taverner." About Dr. Taverner she says, "'Dr. Taverner' will no doubt be recognized by some of my readers, his mysterious nursing home was an actual fact. . . To 'Dr. Taverner' I owe the greatest debt of my life." Who was he?

I have a cassette tape player and I will be looking forward to the first tape.

Two months passed and I didn't receive a reply or the promised tapes so I sent the following letter to him:

6/11/73

Dear Mr. Butler:

I haven't heard from you for some time so am assuming the tapes will be along soon. I am hoping we can make some progress over the summer as I would like to get to England in the fall to see you.

The most important thing for me to know is what Dion Fortune was like when you knew her. Her personality flashes here and there throughout her books but I can never grasp the whole, real person. Also, if she is including bits of other people in her characters, as I'm sure she is, this makes getting the whole picture all the more difficult. Kenneth Grant claims that Vivian/Lilith Le Fay Morgan was modeled on Maiya Tranchell-Hayes (p. 177 *Magical Revival*) but *she* says in the introduction to *Moon Magic* (p. 9) "there is admittedly a great deal of me in Lilith Le Fay" and I certainly feel there is and in many of her other characters. I am curious also about Maiya Tranchell-Hayes, who she was and what was her relationship with D.F.? and also about Chapter X "The Death of Vivien Le Fay Morgan" in *Aspects of Occultism*, who wrote it and who are the personages involved. I assume Lena Rees is supposed to be Moina Mathers. What about Anita Warburn? And was there a Malcolm or Wilfred or are they composites of real people?

Is it true that Dion Fortune neglected to find a successor for her work and is that part of the reason why the Inner Light fell away from its original purpose? What was its original purpose?

I also can't figure out why D. F. never had a child. Did she feel that as an "initiate" she should not so as to give more energy to the Work? Or were there more mundane reasons? Vivien Le Fay Morgan wouldn't marry or have children for just this reason but many of her other characters do and then there is this from *The Winged Bull*: [p. 322]

> A real marriage, which has a spiritual side as well as a physical, ought to put one in circuit with the whole universe, for one becomes a channel for the life of the race going on; that is why there is no blessing on a marriage when you close the gates of life permanently against incoming souls.

I have read *Esoteric Philosophy of Love and Marriage* and studied the love relationships in all of her novels but can't seem to find D. F.'s own orientation. I am also sure D. F.'s relationship with Penry Evans played a key part in her development but exactly how and why I don't know. I would be very much interested to learn more about all this.

I would also like to know where you fit into the picture. Were you ever in the Golden Dawn? How did you meet Dion Fortune? Did Dion Fortune become more extroverted over the years as Kenneth Grant says and were there other changes in her personality that you were aware of? And if you will—what changes did she effect in *you*?

I'll stop here for now. If you could drop me a note as to when I might expect the tapes, I would greatly appreciate it.

Sincerely,

Janine

Chapter 2

MR. BUTLER'S VOICE
FROM ACROSS THE OCEAN

In July of 1973, I finally received a 90-minute cassette recording from Mr. Butler. It was a thrill to hear his voice coming to me across the ocean, speaking of people long dead. It was especially thrilling to hear him talk about Dion Fortune, that wonderful woman I so admired and whom he had known personally.

Following is a complete transcription of the tape except for two or three passages that Mr. Butler said were too personal to be published. His voice was elderly, kindly, with an accent he later explained as being from the Yorkshire area of England. He answered all of my questions in detail and included a great deal of interesting biographical information about himself as well.

My dear friend. Many thanks for your letter. I'm sorry I haven't answered it ere this, but I've been very, very busy indeed, and part of the time I've been ill. For during an illness—I had a very bad touch of bronchitis with a slight touch of pneumonia, which is not too good—and of course what happens as always when I'm ill is that the correspondence piles up on the desk, and when I return I very often seem to have lost track of it. I have to go through it again to find out just where I am, and so letters get mislaid and they wait until they're found again, I'm afraid. But that's the trouble. I've got some [inaudible] at the moment and as I say with illness and the fact that I'm 75, it makes it a bit more difficult for me to do what I want to do. However, here we are. So I'm going to try to answer your letter now on this tape, and then I'll follow this with another tape later on.

You say that it's important for you to know what Dion Fortune was like when I knew her. Well, I knew her over a period of years and her personality was one of those things which was constantly changing. She was a changeable person in the sense that she adapted herself with an uncanny power to the prevailing conditions. She had a chameleon-like tendency at times, and she was capable of seeing things from so many different points of view—so much so that some people thought that perhaps she was only shallow in her views, but actually she wasn't. Underneath the changeable personality there was the fixed rock of the individual self, and that didn't change for the whole time that *I* knew her, and that was from 1925 until her death. But the personality very often did change because she wasn't afraid to confess that on occasion she could be wrong, and when she said so, she investigated the field in which she had found herself to be wrong, and if she found that a certain line of her thinking or of her writing had been incorrect, she didn't cover it up, she didn't sweep it under the carpet, she simply acknowledged that she had been wrong in that, and she went ahead with what she now thought to be the correct line—which is why quite a lot of people got the idea that she was not entirely stable. But she was—eminently so—more so than most people *I've* ever met. But the personality adapted itself to changing conditions and to changing views and to changing aspects of truth. It was not a static thing, it was not a concrete thing, it was a flexible thing, capable of change.

You say, "Is she including bits of other people in her characters?" Yes, of course, of course she did. Actually, a good deal of Vivien Le Fay *was* modeled on Mrs. Tranchell-Hayes, so that Grant was right there. But there was a good deal of her also in it, as she says. And in some of the other parts of her books, you'll find again, that she is projecting herself—very strongly.

Now, you say you're curious about Mrs. Tranchell-Hayes. Well, Mrs. Tranchell-Hayes was the wife of a doctor in the Midlands, originally. She joined the Golden Dawn under the auspices of Dr. Brodie-Innes—of Mr. Brodie-Innes—who was one of the Golden Dawn founders, as you know, and she was his pupil. She worked in Stella Matutina, and when Dion Fortune entered Stella Matutina after she had been thrown out from the Golden Dawn by Mrs. MacGregor Mathers, she came under the tuition of Mrs. Tranchell-Hayes who taught her ABF right from the beginning, renewed her ideas. For although she had just come into the Golden Dawn and its affiliated movement, the Stella Matutina, Dion Fortune had a fair experience before then, and as a psychic she had entered in the very curious college of Dr. Taverner, and

Dr. Taverner was not a fictitious person. Neither was he molded on Dr. Evans, her husband, nor upon Dr. Tranchell-Hayes, who was the husband of Mrs. Tranchell-Hayes.

Now Regardie somewhere refers to Mrs. Tranchell-Hayes. I'll try and get the thing and read it to you because it'll help. Here we are; this is the paragraph I was trying to get for you:

> About 1931 Mrs. Tranchell-Hayes was married to a psychiatrist who practiced in a mental hospital in Worcester. Crowley had occasionally corresponded from France with an astrologer in London by the name of Gabriel Dee. She was a pretty shrewd woman and suffered from no delusions relative to Crowley himself. After I met Gabriel Dee and became good friends, she introduced me to Mrs. Hayes. There must have been some half dozen times when we were invited up to Worcester from London for a dinner and a long evening of interesting conversation. Her psychiatrist husband on one occasion taught me hypnotism, which I have since incorporated into my current professional armamentarium, and I have thought fondly of both of the Hayes on many an occasion. After the death of her husband, she moved down to London.

And here is another bit of information which I got about Mrs. Tranchell-Hayes. This is from an article which appeared in the Spiritualist paper, *Light*, in, I think, 1960 or thereabouts. He's talking about Dion Fortune.

> It was my friend, the late Mrs. Tranchell-Hayes, who told me of her passing. I had become acquainted with this lady through a mutual friend some time previously. She's an important link in the present story for she was able to fill up gaps in the knowledge I had gathered concerning Dion Fortune's pilgrimage, and she was herself a walking encyclopedia of occult knowledge. She possessed a remarkable collection of books and manuscripts on sorcery, necromancy, and all ungodliness and exercised as well a benevolent sway over a flat, first in Kingston House and later in the privacy of Kensington

Square, bedecked with witches' rosaries, a finery of occult amulets and charms, and some very effective representations of power-charged ancient imagery. Later still, she was to become the presiding hostess of a small group of which I was a member for the weekly discussion of subjects of a supernormal character. Dr. Sherwood-Taylor, Director of the Science Museum, my friends Margery Bowen and Charles Richard Cammell added their weight among others to the elucidation of occult and magical problems. Mrs. Tranchell-Hayes had known Dion Fortune intimately since the latter was a girl. She had detected in her, from the start, an individual of strong and talented personality, a poetess of great charm and distinction, and a potential occultist of discernment and cultivation in her chosen province. Dion Fortune, who embodied the intriguing personality of Mrs. Tranchell-Hayes in one of the most powerful of her novels, *The Sea Priestess*, hailed originally from Llandudno where her parents, I believe, managed a high-class hotel. Mrs. Hayes spoke with great admiration of Dion Fortune's mother who she said had been a most cultivated and religious woman and had imprinted in her daughter the principle of the Christian Science creed. Dion Fortune often confessed to me that she owed her own, lifelong interest in regenerative powers of the mind to an early absorption of the teachings of Mrs. Baker-Eddy.

That's slightly incorrect. Dion Fortune did not hail from Llandudno, although her mother did keep a boardinghouse there, a high-class boardinghouse. But she hailed from the Sheffield area, and was a member of the Firth family, the stainless steel people. By the way, I see that somebody, one of the so-called authorities, has said that she was an orphan, that she was under guardians. But she wasn't. She was under her mother.

Now, another thing is that Mrs. Tranchell-Hayes gained contact with Dion Fortune simply because of the fact that she had joined the Stella Matutina, but before Dion Fortune joined the Stella Matutina she had a rather checkered psychic career, which I'll tell you about later. However, let's carry on:

> The other woman (that is, Mrs. Tranchell-Hayes) had become the younger's guide, philosopher, and friend in the affairs of the spirit, equipped with wider experience and a more extensive knowledge. She had, by her advice and stimulus, encouraged Dion to bring out the best that was in her as regards occult powers. Mrs. Hayes, among her other qualifications, was the widow of an eminent psychiatrist and while residing with her husband in a big mental home near Northampton—

I'm not so certain where it was, whether it was Worcester or Northampton. I think it might have been Worcester rather than Northampton.

> —of which he was Director, she had availed herself of the opportunity of studying the various forms of derangement which came under her husband's care and had built up therefrom a very respectable acquaintance with the body-mind relationship with all its psychological and pathological complications.

Colin Wilson once said that Dr. Taverner was no more than Dr. Hayes. That isn't so at all. Dr. Taverner was a person in his own right, and when I come to give you the beginning of Dion Fortune's occult work, I'll tell you more about him. But, so far I want to keep to answering your letter as it is. I can go further later.

Now, yes, Lena Rees is Mrs. Mathers. Anita Warburn I don't know anything at all about. And I don't know anything of a Malcolm or a Wilfred. I think they're composites, rather.

Now it's quite true that Dion Fortune did neglect to find a successor for her work, and that is part of the reason why the Inner Light fell away from its original purpose. Yes, I agree with you. I don't suppose the Inner Light would agree with you, but I do. I think it is correct. I'm still a member of the Inner Light but at the same time, although I go with it because I can do so quite nicely, I'd like to end up my incarnation still in this fraternity, which has meant so much to me through the years—although at the present time it has very little which really helps me. I suppose that's my fault because they're still teaching. But nevertheless, they did diverge from the path which Dion Fortune had mapped out for the Society—or for the fraternity in the beginning. They call themselves a Society now. It's much more respectable. But we were a fraternity. We had an outer aspect, the Society of the Inner Light, yes, but all those who joined it and became workers in it, became the Fraternity of the Inner Light. We were a brotherhood—not a society.

This chap, Bernard Bromage, has written an article, which incidentally, I'll be sending you.[1] It's my only copy, so let me have it back, but I think it will help you if you don't take the writer too much at the foot of the letter. He wasn't always correct in what he said. There are several points which I would query. In fact, I've marked them. So you'll be able to use it as an interesting indication—not as absolute truth always. He's talking about 3 Queensborough Terrace, which was the center from which we worked in London. He says:

> There were secrets within secrets in this institution. I was given an opportunity to meet several of the students and to learn how their individual needs were catered for by special courses, adapted to what Dion Fortune regarded as their grade of spiritual development. There was a Grail chapel. There was, I think, a kind of intermediate department for the Cabalistically inclined. There was a department for initiates given over, I understood, to research into the higher realms of occultism.

Fairly true, but he's only got the outside picture of it. Dion Fortune didn't confide all that to him, I think, but she used him for her own particular purpose, and he never realized that he only saw the outside angle. Nevertheless, his article is fairly good. He talks here about *The Secrets of Dr. Taverner*, and he says that:

> She, working in collaboration with her husband, had handled and cured some very severe cases of collapse caused by what used to be known as diabolical agency— serious obsessions, admitted by all competent authorities to be the most difficult things in the world to treat. She

---

[1] The article that he sent me was titled "Dion Fortune," from the 1960 spring issue of *Light*.

had, by the application of her own technique, banished
to where they belonged . . . .

Now that was true, but she was working with Dr. Evans then in the
light of her own knowledge of the work which Dr. Taverner had
put in and with her knowledge too of the work of Dr. Tranchell-
Hayes so that she was using a composite again there. But she wrote
The Secrets of Dr. Taverner before she had any real contact with her
husband, Dr. Penry Evans. It was one of the first of her novels. The
first one was *Demon Lover* and the second one was *The Secrets of Dr.
Taverner*.

Now, I'll just answer the rest of your letter and then I'll try to
give you something about her very early days—as far as I know
them, of course. You ask, "What was the original purpose of the
Inner Light?" It was a school of initiation, no less, and it could
deliver the goods. It was not a case of jam yesterday, jam tomorrow, but never jam today. Those who were ready for it got jam
today, and we saw, positively, what occultism really was—something which the modern Inner Light student never sees because
that's gone now, gone entirely. It was due, of course, to the fact
that Dion Fortune was a most peculiar person. She was like HPB
(Madame Blavatsky), and she had powers which Madame
Blavatsky also possessed.

You say you can't figure out why they never had a child.
Hmmm. Well, Vivien Le Fay Morgan gives the key to that and, of
course, you say—you quote from *The Winged Bull* there—that's
true, about the gates of life being barred against incoming souls,
yes—"there's no blessing on a marriage"—well look at it this way.
It might be that in one incarnation, children—the path of the
Hearth-Fire—was not the path. It certainly wasn't for Dion Fortune.
And if we say "there is no blessing on a marriage when you close
the gates of life permanently," well that was certainly true with
regard to Dion Fortune. Her marriage was most unhappy, or
became most unhappy.

Now, I'll try and get some more about the relationship
between herself and Penry Evans. I'm trying to get in contact with
someone who was in the Lodge in the early days and knew something about that, and if I can get hold of him I'll see if I can arrange
for you to see him and have a chat with him about the thing—you'll

get another angle on Dion Fortune. And then I have another lady who used to be at a training college with Dion Fortune when she was Violet Firth and who also could give you some points. I'm also going to try and get her to meet you if I can.

And where do I fit into the picture? No, I was never in the Golden Dawn. And how did I meet Dion Fortune? Well, I'll tell you on the other side of this.

Yes, she did become more extroverted as the years went by. And there were changes. Her personality became in some ways more fixed along the outer levels; it became more fluid, it's curious.

And you ask, finally, "What changes did she effect in you?"— that is, myself. Well, I'll tell when we get down to it. But what I say to you is distinctly sub rosa—a matter of personal experience which I don't want proclaimed from the housetops, and I haven't told many people about it except those whom I could trust. However—

Nevertheless, I shall look forward to seeing you. But I should like some fairly firm idea when you're likely to be over here. September is out absolutely. The whole of September is out because I shall not be available to anyone during September. Anyway, you can let me know the definite date; then I'll make arrangements so that we can have a really good talk over these matters.

Now I want to talk about the question you asked about my own contact with the Golden Dawn and with the Inner Light. No, I was never in the Golden Dawn except that when Dion Fortune's own fraternity, the Inner Light, was founded we were in close touch with Stella Matutina, so much so that Stella Matutina abetted our rituals and at various times they visited us, as senior brethren. When we sat in Lodge, very often there would be senior brethren behind a curtain. And they were, we understood, members of Stella Matutina, the Bristol Lodge, but come over to listen to our workings. But I myself was never in the Golden Dawn.

Now, you ask how did I come into the Inner Light. Now that's a long story and I'm going to try and answer it on this particular tape so that you'll get the basis of what actually happened. It may be useful in future years when I've passed to other realms of existence because this is the authentic material, straight from the horse's mouth, as we say.

Well now, I'd better go back a considerable time. I'd better give you actually a whole, the idea of the whole of my life, the early part of my life at all events, so you may get a clear picture. And I'll leave it to your discretion as to how you use that.

I lived the first part of my life in a little Yorkshire village about fifteen miles from York. I was just an ordinary kid, I suppose, except that I had an awful desire to know—to know—I was the real inquisitive one, you know, I was the elephant's child. I possessed an insatiable curiosity, but I didn't do much schooling because every year, in the winter, I went down with either bronchitis, pneumonia, double pneumonia, inflammation of the lungs. I ran the changes on those. And every year practically, I was out of action for about six or seven months. The end result was that I had possibly about three or four years actual instruction at school before I left my Yorkshire village when I was 12. I left it then in order to be given a trade training at a charity school down in the south of England.

So then, we went to this charity school and I learned a trade. From there I went out into the hard world and was earning my living during the beginning of the war, and then later on I joined up and served in France, but the rest I'll tell you in a moment.

But to come back to my Yorkshire village. I wrote a story called "The Mound on the Moor," which appeared in the first number of a now defunct occult magazine—what the devil is the name of it now?—*New Dimensions*, and this particular story gave my first occult experience. I was very fond of reading. I read everything— everything I could get my hands on—and in those Yorkshire villages in those days there was remarkably little. I remember reading through a whole series of magazines and *Windsor Magazine*, and others which I had coaxed from some of the villagers, but generally speaking it was very, very difficult running.

However, one magazine I did get hold of had a story of someone who had read about the classical sacrifices and had full details of how they were conducted. But somehow or other this attracted me tremendously, this idea of offering sacrifice to the gods was something which was very attractive. So I—one Saturday—I took some paper and some matches and I knew where I was bound for and that was a tumulus which was in the forest a little distance away, about a mile away from the village. So down I went to the tumulus, got on its summit. There was an old rock there, which I used as my altar. I lit my papers and put some wood on it and then I got hold of some of the weed which was round about and put it on the top to make a joyful smoke before the Lord. And I said my piece as I had memorized it—because I had a good memorizing faculty always. I said my piece and I invoked the gods.

Now, it was a lovely sunny day, not a cloud in sight. Yet, quite suddenly, the sky began to darken. It was as though an impalpable veil began to build up between me and the sun, and, although it was a brilliant summer day, I was cold. And I began to get frightened. And more and more of this kind of dusk came down between myself and the sun. More and more I felt cold. More and more I felt frightened. Until at last, with a mighty wrench, I tore myself away from in front of the altar and head over heels I fell down the side of the tumulus, whereupon everything was all right. The sun was shining its full blaze. It was very, very hot. The only thing was, it was a very frightened little boy of 9 years old who was sitting at the bottom of the tumulus wondering what had happened. Well, I ought to have been scared at that. I *was* scared at the time. But it didn't stop me. I was like the elephant's child, still full of insatiable curiosity. But one thing I *had* proved to myself— that there was something beyond the material, and that vague feeling which I had occasionally in church—especially during the Holy Communion—was real. There was something beyond the material.

Now when I went down to the charity school, that was run on old army lines, the lines of the army of the Boer War, and believe me, discipline was applied. Oh dear, wasn't it! And I had very little time for mystical or esoteric ideas. My job was living and keeping my nose above water in the competitive gang of 200 boys from all levels who were mainly—as it seemed to me—mainly occupied in trying to make my life a misery. And it was a misery for quite a time until I began to readjust myself. And then, in the school library one Good Friday, I was reading something or other and I came cross Prentiss Mulfred's book, one of the New Thought books, and that started a train of thought in my mind. But again, I didn't carry it any further, but it lay there, latent.

Well, when I left this particular school and started work, I was working—this was just the beginning of the war—I was working in the munition works and one of the men there—people came from all over the place—one of the men there had been a traveling mesmerist going about from show to show, doing mesmeric entertainments. They're forbidden now by law but in those days they were a great thing, and I cottoned on to this chap. I was very interested with him and when he found that I had had this particular experience, he began to open out. Well, he taught me how to use a mesmeric technique, how to act as subject, how to act as operator, and he gave me a really thorough grounding in the subjects of mesmerism and hypnotism, which are two distinct things, incidentally. And then one day he says, "Well, there are a lot of people, not so far away, at Wimbledon, who know a lot about these things. They're called Spiritualists." And he told me how to reach this place. So I cycled down from Weybridge where I was working and made the acquaintance of the Spiritualists and this was what I wanted. Here was some living contact with another plane of life. So I fell into it like a kid into a treacle barrel. But after a time, I began to get dissatisfied. There wasn't enough here; something was missing. I wanted more, and I didn't get it from the trance-control addresses of the mediums, I didn't get it from the casual psychic phenomena. Incidentally, I began to develop psychic phenomena hand over fist at that time. But I wasn't satisfied.

And then, one Sunday, the president of this particular society said, "Well, next Sunday we have as our speaker Mr. Robert King. There will be no clairvoyance." Well, of course, clairvoyance at the end of every Spiritualist address was common, and is common today, and if it wasn't for the clairvoyance you'd find half the Spiritualist churches empty. But anyway, I thought, "Well, I don't know. I'll come down and hear what he has to say. Perhaps I may get some ideas." So the following Sunday, away I set on my bike and I arrived down there. And a bearded man got on the platform, and he looked across at me, and I looked across at him, and that was that.

He was speaking about the symbol of the circle and the cross, and I think I held my breath for about three quarters of an hour. I was on an edge of a chair, simply staring at that man, listening. If I had four ears I'd have had them all in operation at that time, listening in to what he was saying. This was what I'd been looking for. This was It, with a capital *I*.

Well, after he had finished on the platform, he came off to get a glass of hot milk that was always given to the speaker after the address. They had a glass of hot milk before they departed. But he didn't get to his glass of hot milk before I was there. I grabbed the lapel of his coat and I said, "When can I see you? I *must* see you." I was absolutely raving, and I felt almost mad over it. I *must* see this man. This is the man I *must* see. I must talk to him. He looked at me. He said, "Yes," he said, "we've met before, you know. All right." And he fixed a time up for me to see him and where I had to go. And that was my first introduction to my first teacher, Robert King.

Through him I came in contact with, not only the Theosophical movement, but also with an active inner group of which he was one of the heads, and that inner group is one to which I still belong and have belonged ever since that time, ever since 1915. It had nothing to do with the Inner Light as such, but it is one of the basic groups which exists behind a good many of these fraternities and orders.

So that's how I came really into the occult movement. You see, I'd had the intimations of it with me the whole time but now I was put on the Path. It was about that time that I had my first conscious astral projection, assisted by the power of Robert King. He put me out of my body, and I saw for myself for the first time something of the conditions of the Inner Planes. And I learned by practical experience that I was not my body, but I was that which used the body. That is the central plank upon which everything else has been built.

Then, of course, I joined up. I don't know why I did it. I think I felt fed up one Saturday evening. And I was intensely patriotic and still am, for the matter of that. So I thought I might as well join up and help the war efforts. Which I did. And then after 1918, after the armistice, I came back—I was invalided back from France—and went to a military hospital in the north of England where again I met Robert King, who was up lecturing on the Liberal Catholic Church to which I belonged. Because he was one of its leaders, I joined it under his auspices in 1915.

Then I went out to India, and I spent some years there. I came in contact with a group of yogis from whom I learned much. I've worked with them, and I learned much from them. I have traveled over the length and breadth of India. I was on the Indian Telegraph Department, seconded from my regiment, and I saw all things. I saw the good side of the Hindu idea and the bad side. I saw, yes, I saw things I can't describe really because they're indescribable. I've been in a town where the people were dying by the hundreds who were simply lying in the streets in bunches, all dying. Starvation—people don't realize what it is. They may read about it in the papers, but to see it actually happening—men, women, and children—it's ghastly.

And then I saw the other side. I saw the conditions of the ruling classes, not merely the British. The British raj did a good job. They did their best to help the poor people, they did their best to give justice. But they were up against a landed aristocracy—the princes—and they were up against the peculiar communal system, which can very often be a real death-dealer, especially in places like India. And I saw some of that aspect of it. But I also came in touch with the Lords of Wisdom, with the Masters of the Path. Concerning that I can't say anything. But nevertheless, I did. By that time I was in the Theosophical Society and I thought well, I might as well join what they call the Inner Section of the Theosophical Society. So I put in my application.

Quite a long time after I put in this application, I heard nothing. I was at the time at a place called Muttra, which was at the edge of the Sinn Desert and the last place that Alexander the Great's army reached in its penetration of India. I'm not at all surprised they went back. There was sand in all directions. However, I went down with a terrific attack of malarial fever and malaria can be pretty devastating. As a matter of fact, it gave me very bad heart trouble, and that is really one of the things from which I suffer today.

However, I was just getting better from this malarial attack, sitting up and taking nourishment, and one day one of the Hindu people in the hospital, one of the servants, he said, "Oh, there's a Mme. Sahib wants to see you." I said, "Oh, does she?" I said, "All right, show her in." So into the ward came a lady, and she said, "I don't suppose you know me?"

I said, "No, I don't."

"Well," she said, "I'm the corresponding secretary of the esoteric section of the Theosophical Society, Miss A. J. Wilson."

I said, "Oh, yes." I thought, "Oh, here it is. I'm going to be given my permission to join the Inner Section."

She said, "You know, some time ago you put in an application for membership of the Inner Section, the Esoteric Section of the Theosophical Society."

I said, "Yes."

"Well," she said, "I've now got the reply. The outer head (that's Dr. Besant, Annie Besant) says that the Inner Chiefs, the inner heads, that is to say the Masters who are behind the Esoteric Section, the Masters say that on no account whatsoever are you to be allowed into the Esoteric Section."

And that was that! Woe was me! I think my heart went right down to where my boots would have been if I'd had them on. However, there it was. It was quite definite. You couldn't have it much more final than that: "On no account!" And it was the Masters behind the Esoteric Section who said it. Oh well, that was it.

"However," she went on, "I've brought you this." And she brought out a deep red rose and gave it to me.

I thought to myself, "Well, that's very kind of you but it doesn't help me very much." However, I said, "Thank you very much. " And away she went.

Well, I came back from India and I was still in the service, in the Royal Engineers because I had transferred from my former unit, and I went to Gosport, near Southampton, and there I met the girl who I married some time later, and, with its usual tact, six weeks after we were married the army transferred me right away from Southampton. It's a trick they have. And I found myself at Algerthorpe. Well, I was there some time. And then I was transferred down to a place called Chepstow, down on the River Severn, and I had to be instructor to boys in the army who were training to be tradesmen-electricians.

Well, my wife was still in Southampton. And she sent me one day a copy of the *Occult Review,* and in this review there was an article on magic by Dion Fortune. I read the article and it rang bells! In every direction! *This* was what I wanted. At the time I couldn't get hold of Robert King. He was out of the country at the time and abroad. But anyway, I wrote to Dion Fortune through the editor of the *Occult Review,* and she wrote back and said that she had a center at Glastonbury and if I cared to go down there, she could see me there. Well, I wasn't so far from Glastonbury. I had to cross the Bristol Channel and get down to Bristol and then go from Bristol down to Glastonbury. So down I went. I got a weekend pass and I started off on my odyssey. I got down to Glastonbury and I asked the man who was the combined station master, train driver, ticket collector, and guard when the train went back. I said, "What train is there back to Bristol tonight? What train leaves here tonight?"

"Oh, there's a 6:30, sir." Well that was all right because it was about 1:00. So I ambled up to the town and found where the Chalice Orchard was, and Chalice Orchard was the center of Dion Fortune's work in Glastonbury. I'll tell you more about that later. However, up to Chalice Orchard I went, and I was met by Dion Fortune and by her right-hand man, a man called Mr. C. T. Loveday. And during the conversation I told them the story of the refusal of the Inner Chiefs of the Theosophical Society to allow me to go into the Esoteric Section, whereupon Loveday went away and came back. He said, "Have you seen this before?" And he showed me a cross, and on the cross was a rose. I said, "Yes, of course I have. I've seen that. Robert King wears a cross like that. It's a rosy cross." He said, "Yes, it is." And quite suddenly I realized what he was driving at. Dion Fortune was grinning like a Cheshire cat. She said, "Yes," she said, "Now you know why they refused you. They refused you because you didn't belong to their school. They knew which school you belong to. You belong to the Western tradition, not the Eastern." And from that day onwards, I was in.

I joined the group. I'd been duly initiated into the first three degrees. And I began to see something of what went on in the Lodge. I helped in various things in the Lodge. And so it continued right away through until the war broke out in 1939. I had at that time founded another Lodge, which was contacted on to Dion Fortune's Lodge at 3 Queensborough Terrace in London. She had given me permission to do so. She gave me the contact and abetted the ritual, which I made for myself. So I worked this particular Inner Light Lodge at Guildford until, I think it was, 1941.

Then war reasons made it imperative that we close down. Nevertheless, I kept in contact more or less, but I didn't get up to London very often so I couldn't see the later days of Dion Fortune, except I did hear how she was getting on. I did hear some of the yarns concerning her. For instance, they were bombed at 3 Queensborough Terrace. A bomb dropped straight down in the building. And Dion Fortune was having a bath at the time. She'd just come out of the bath and she was standing more or less in the altogether, just with a towel draped around her, and there was a terrific crash and the bathroom behind her simply disappeared down into the basement. She was left standing. She didn't worry. It didn't worry her one iota. She was above that kind of thing. Anyway, as I say, I didn't see much of her and then later I heard that she had passed over. Just for the record, she passed over from leukemia. She'd had a tooth badly extracted and somehow or other leukemia set in and she died. I think it was the "Butcher's Shovel" we call it, St. Mary's, Paddington where she passed over. But quite definitely she died of leukemia. I've heard idiotic yarns that she was trying black magical operations and that the forces had recoiled upon her, and all the rest of the nonsense which you get around these things. But that is how she died—leukemia. And that is where she died—in London. Her body was taken down to Glastonbury for burial, and it was buried in Glastonbury Cemetery and you can see the headstone there today. And her right-hand man, Mr. Loveday, died in 1947, and he, too—he was buried next to her.

Things have gone through many vicissitudes since then because when Loveday and Dion Fortune both passed over, things began to be carefully altered. And so the fraternity diverged from the former policy.

So now you know how I came into it, how I met Dion Fortune, and I think you'll agree that it was planned somehow. Every link in that chain holds true, right away through, that I should have these experiences and I should end up in Dion Fortune's school.

Well, now I think that is all I can tell you of that at the moment. I've one particular thing I do want to tell you and that is of present conditions, and then you'll get a clear picture of where I stand. Some members of the Society of the Inner Light, disagreeing with the new slant, began to express their disapproval by leaving, and in Francis King's *Ritual Magic in England*, you'll find some details of those members. One of the groups, which is the larger group he mentions, formed the Helios Book Service, which sold secondhand books and new books dealing with occult subjects. And I was associated with the beginnings of that, connected with Mr. John Hall, who is the Managing Director, and Mr. Basil Wilby, both of whom had been in the Inner Light in fairly high positions.

Well, now they had an idea that they would issue a Kabbalistic correspondence course, which they did. But after six or seven lessons they found it difficult to do the ordinary work and also run the course, so they asked me if I would take it over. I took it over and I am now the Director of Studies and the head of the Cabalistic Course, which is distributed by Helios but which was compiled by me.[2] The first seven lessons were compiled by Mr. Wilby, and the remaining forty-three were compiled by me. But my contact with Dion Fortune had meant this, that the old contact I had way back with Robert King in the Egyptian days in the Lodge which he was working with at that time, it meant that the old teacher who was there, and to whom I'd been linked, now took over again and became my teacher.

Robert King himself passed over and Dion Fortune passed over. I was left. But a man whom I call "The Opener of the Ways"— that's the title we give him, "The Opener of the Ways"—he took me on again. I'd never been really out of his orbit. I'd forgotten about him in all the excitement of things. But anyway, I was within his orbit again and I was working for him and so I am today. And this work of the Helios correspondence course is done under his aegis and with his advice. So that's how we stand today. Any queries you want to make about that, I'll try and answer them as fully as I can. Oh, and by the way, you will have noticed that my dialect is rather curious. I am an Englishman, but I have a distinct dialect in my voice. That is because, although I left Yorkshire when I was 12, I've never lost the Yorkshire dialect, the Yorkshire sound of my voice. So you've got to put up with that. Everyone has.

Now, as you will see, there are gaps in my knowledge. I was very closely connected with Dion Fortune in some ways, at certain times. But there were other times when I was not in her vicinity, and therefore there are things about her which I don't know—quite a lot. But what I'm going to try to do is to get all the

---

[2] Helios Book Service, the publishing company organized by a number of now famous students from the esoteric world, is no longer in existence. People interested in the books they published on occult subjects should search secondhand bookstores.

people who do know about her behavior and were living at that time and see if they can give you some other information also. It'll take a little time perhaps, but I think I can manage to get them to give us some of their ideas. In the meantime, I'm sending you this manuscript which was written by a man who has passed over now, and although it's not entirely correct—there are several errors in it—it's quite good. And I'll mark out where the errors come.

I think that is all for the time. I'll send you another tape as soon as I can get the time to make one for you, giving you some further details. In the meantime, if there's any point which you wish to ask me any questions on, please let me have it as soon as possible and I'll reply. I think that is all. Cheerio.

Chapter 3

KENNETH GRANT
AND ISRAEL REGARDIE

At this point I was very pleased with how things were going, so I decided to be a little more daring. Kenneth Grant had mentioned in his book, *The Magical Revival*, that he had been present at two meetings between Dion Fortune and Aleister Crowley.

Kenneth Grant studied magic under Aleister Crowley and served as Crowley's secretary during the period just before Crowley's death. In collaboration with John Symonds, he edited and annotated several of Crowley's major works. *The Magical Revival* traces the magical "current" employed by Aleister Crowley, Dion Fortune and others to its roots in the Tantric Tradition of the Far East and other ancient cults. The primary element in these cults was ritual magic involving sex between the priest and the priestess.

Personally, although I respected the Tantric system, my opinion of Aleister Crowley was and is decidedly less neutral. In any event, I did not feel an affinity towards that path. Nevertheless, I felt it necessary to contact Kenneth Grant in order to learn what his impressions of Dion Fortune had been on the two occasions when they met.

On July 1, 1973, I sent the following letter to Mr. Grant in care of his publishers, Frederick Muller.[1]

---

[1] Frederick Muller Limited is now a division of Rider.

Cambridge, Massachusetts
July 1, 1973

Kenneth Grant
c/o Frederick Muller Limited
London,
England

Dear Mr. Grant:

W.E. Butler has suggested I contact you. I am trying to piece together the life of Dion Fortune with the intention of writing her biography and I have learned more details from your chapter in *The Magical Revival* than from any other published source. Mr. Butler knew Dion Fortune from 1925 when she started the Fraternity of the Inner Light until her death and he is preparing tapes for me of his experiences as her student.

It is my understanding from your book that you met Dion Fortune on two occasions and that you saw the letters which passed between her and Crowley. I would greatly appreciate anything more you could recall about these two meetings, when and where they occurred, what was said, and in particular, what Dion Fortune was like. You mention that she became more outgoing as the years went by. Were your two meetings far apart so that you were able to perceive a change or did you hear of it? I would also be interested in your impressions of Penry Evans if you met him as well as anything else you think might be relevant.

I will be looking forward to hearing from you.

Sincerely,

Janine Chapman

The next day I sent a letter to Israel Regardie, who claimed to have spent a weekend with Dion Fortune and her husband in 1933.[2] Mr. Regardie studied with Aleister Crowley and was his personal secretary for many years. He had written many books on various aspects of ceremonial magic and was most famous for publishing *The Complete Golden Dawn System of Magic*.[3]

Following is the letter I sent to him and the responses I received from Mr. Grant and Mr. Regardie.

Cambridge, Massachusetts
July 2, 1973

Israel Regardie
c/o Llewellyn Publications
St. Paul, Minnesota 55165

Dear Mr. Regardie:

For several years the quality and objectivity of your writings have been one of the chief motivating factors in keeping me at my occult studies where I found so much to disgust and discourage me and when I began to wonder if my abilities were not wasted in this pursuit. I have not written to you before this because I had no reason to but I have a special favor to ask of you now.

I reached the occult via an interest in Symbolist art and literature begun in college. For three years I studied with Ophiel, doing all the work in all of his

---

[2] Israel Regardie, *The Eye in the Triangle* (Phoenix, AZ: New Falcon Press, 1982), p. 114.

[3] Israel Regardie, *The Complete Golden Dawn System of Magic* (Phoenix, AZ: New Falcon Press, 1984.

courses and books. I am enclosing a copy of an article I wrote during that time for *Gnostica News*, the occult magazine put out by Llewellyn Publications.

The strongest influence on my work has come from the books of Dion Fortune, perhaps because she is the only writer in the tradition who was also a woman. Her words have had a personal relevance for me that no other writer's have ever had and I have adopted the standards outlined in *Training and Work of an Initiate* as my own. It would be a valuable lesson for me to learn the details of her development as an occultist. For this reason, and because I feel her life could be a model to other women, I have undertaken to write her biography. I began reading for this project in January of '72 and as part of the preparation I have been working through the Golden Dawn system under the direction of one of your former students. I am in contact with W. E. Butler in England who knew Dion Fortune from 1925 when she started the Fraternity of the Inner Light until her death. He has offered to give me whatever information he has concerning her and is preparing tapes for me of his experiences as her student.

It is my understanding, from what you say in *The Eye in the Triangle* that you spent a weekend with Dion Fortune and her husband in or around 1933. I am also assuming from this paragraph that you had met her on one previous occasion and that this weekend was your last encounter with both her and Penry Evans. I would greatly appreciate anything more you could remember about this weekend, especially about Dion Fortune herself, what she was like, what her house was like, what you discussed, and anything else you think might be relevant.

I will be looking forward to hearing from you.

Janine Chapman

9 Aug 73 e.v.

Dear Ms. Chapman:

Do what thou wilt shall be the whole of the Law!
I am so glad you found something of use in my
chapter on Dion. Apart from what I wrote there, and
my article on her which appeared in 'Man, Myth &
Magic', I have only my own impressions of her, and a
few things I have heard about her.

I met her in 1945. She was close to death and had
lost much of the physical force and vigour that is so
apparent in the photograph which accompanied my
article. Even so, she conveyed (*transmitted*, would be a
better word) a tremendous psychic vitality which
struck me very forcibly at the time, although in those
days I was not so sensitive to individual presences as I
now am. It was obvious to me then, and the conviction
grows stronger each time I read anything by her, that
Dion saw herself as *the* magical shakti of the New
Aeon. Aleister called such avatars of shakti, *scarlet
women*, and although Dion was far from fulfilling this
role in quite the same way that most of Aleister's
shaktis fulfilled it, she was, I believe, fully conscious of
her magical abilities in this direction. Her novel, *Moon
Magic*, confirms this, and I will remember her zest in
discussing with Aleister the possibility of reviving the
pagan attitudes to cosmic and elemental forces.

She was very partial to the idea of Power and I
have heard it said that she was a very dominating
woman who did not scruple to tell her followers how
they should arrange their private lives—sometimes
with disastrous results.

T. Penry Evans, a Welsh physician and a psychic,
kept very much in the background, and it is said that
Dion henpecked him unmercifully.

Unfortunately, Dion's papers etc., seem to have fallen into unsympathetic hands and much of her unpublished work, I believe, has been willfully destroyed. This is no doubt due to the fact that during the latter part of her life she grew less reserved about her interest in the 93 Current as represented by THERION and others, and her followers - being mealy-mouthed and afraid to follow any line of thought to its logical conclusion - decided to destroy evidence of what they must have recognized as 'dangerous' teachings. It is a great shame; I saw a large stack of Aleister/Dion letters after his death. They were supposed to be on their way to Aleister's legatee in New York, but I doubt if they ever got there.

More than this I cannot say. I do hope that your book will fill a need, the need that Dion still needs of being placed properly in the perspective of occultore. Perhaps her most significant contribution to the subject lies, as I have intimated in my book, in her calling attention to the *kalas* or magical emanations in their relation to the endocrine system, which in turn relates to the subtle anatomy of the *chakras* and the *Kundalini Shakti*, or Scarlet Woman, as the dormant power in the occult dimensions of man's consciousness. I hope you will emphasize this aspect of her teaching as I think it is paramount.

I wish you all success with your book and if I can be of any further help please do not hesitate to let me know.

Love is the law, love under will.
Yours Fraternally,

Kenneth

7-19-73

Ms. Janine Chapman
Cambridge, Mass. 02140

Dear Janine Chapman:

I have your letter of July 2nd which I found very interesting.

If you are in touch with Mr. Butler in England who has known Dion Fortune from the beginning and has promised to tape for you his experiences relating to her, then you are indeed, very fortunate. He probably is in a better position than almost anyone else, to provide you with the basic material you need for this biography. Also Basil Wilby of Helios.

I met Dion Fortune 40 years ago, immediately after the publication of my two books: "The Garden of Pomegranates" and the "Tree of Life." At that time she was writing her own book, "The Mystical Qabalah" in monthly installments for the periodical which she issued from her own society. I met her a couple of times in Bayswater and then once out in Glastonbury. Unfortunately I was sick on the latter occasion and was in bed during the weekend that I was there, and remember very little about it.

Frankly, 40 years is a long time - and since, in effect, my contact with her was really of the most superficial kind, I cannot say that I recall many details that would be of much value to you in writing a biography. It has only just struck me, that 40 years is one helluva long time! And we never reached a more intimate rapport primarily because I declined to join her Society of the Inner Life. This is not to ascribe petty motives to her, but merely to say, that in effect, there was little to provide us with any deeper intimacy. In point of fact, perhaps the burden of the blame is perhaps on my part. I was once present at her home in Bayswater, having tea with her and her husband, and she "henpecked" him. And so, while I might agree with you or any other critic, that this was pure pettiness on my part, I must register the fact that this stuck "in my craw" - never to be forgotten. It is a minor thing, and of course, something that happens in every marital relationship. But at that time I was a kid and somehow expected more of her. Another recollection I have of her, to offset the bad taste this left in my mouth, is that when I was initiated into the Neophyte degree or grade of the Golden Dawn in Bristol, she was charming enough to have traveled all the way from London to be present at my initiation. It was a charming gesture and I shall always be grateful to her. We probably would have remained *distant* friends forever had it not been for my eventually falling foul with the Chiefs of the Bristol Temple and then deciding to publish the material in decent organized form, which Crowley had failed to do - 25 years earlier. I don't think she ever forgave me anymore than did most of the other members of the Order. And in all fairness to them, I must say, I cannot blame them much.

But there are few details that I can give you about her save that she was a very kind woman and I am sure a very strong and powerful woman. It is too bad she had to marry a relatively short Welshman instead of a husky 7-foot Viking, who might have been of more use to her as a polarity than was Penry Evans. I liked Penry Evans, and we got along relatively well, but he was a very guarded and from my current viewpoint, a very inhibited kind of man, regardless of whether or not he had the psychic abilities so often possessed by the Welsh.

I remember, on one occasion, when I took Evans to meet E. Graham Howe—an English psychiatrist—who was vaguely interested in the Order at that time. It could have been a fascinating meeting, looking at it from the hindsight point of view, but as it seems now, I would say that Evans was very inhibited and abashed and felt in no way the equal - socially, intellectually nor professionally - of Graham Howe; which is why perhaps he suffered himself to be henpecked by this big powerful woman that Dion Fortune really was.

Since you have raised the issue, and while I cannot provide you with any details because of lapse of memory, I am almost inclined to say that I am sorry I never got to know her as well as I might have.

There is a new book extant entitled: "The Magickal Revival" by Kenneth Grant, who is an erstwhile Crowley disciple, who has some very interesting comments to make about Dion Fortune.

He claims, in that book, that she met him and Aleister Crowley probably in the early 40's. This I find rather hard to believe, for one of the few things that I do remember is this: that in my youth I was a very enthusiastic Crowleyite and of course could speak of little else besides the old man, which must have amused her tremendously. She was familiar—though not very deeply, I should say—with some of Crowley's writings, but I am certain she would no more have thought of meeting him than I would now think of flying to the moon. Her phrase might have been "that if you touch pitch, you get dirty". Which, to a large extent, is very true, because most of those who consorted in any way with Crowley, had become contaminated with the same kind of adverse publicity that attended Crowley. And there are only a very few minor exceptions to this. She wanted none of that.

Thank you for your most interesting letter and my most profound regrets that I am unable to be of any greater help than I have been.

I wish you great success in the writing of this biography and do hope that you obtain a very great deal of pleasure from writing it. I think the task needs very much to be done and I do hope that when you have completed it and have it published that you will do me the courtesy of so advising me.

My very best wishes,

Very sincerely yours,

J. S. Regardie

FIR:tw

I wrote the following letters to Mr. Butler and Mr. Grant in October and November of 1973. I was making definite plans to visit England, stay a week, and interview as many people as possible.

Cambridge, Massachusetts
October 29, 1973

Dear Mr. Butler,

I have listened to your first tape several more
times and have made a transcript of it which I will
bring with me when I come in case you want to look
it over. Also, there seems to have been something
erased by mistake at the end of the tape. I'm sending
along a copy of the last part of it so you can see what I
mean.

I was glad to learn that you were always a very
curious person because that should mean that you will
be patient with my own endless questions. In some
instances I realize I may be asking more than you are
willing to give out but I feel I must take the chance of
offending you rather than never have a chance at
knowing. At the same time I feel guilty about putting
you on the spot about intimate subjects.

Recently I have been reading on the subject of
Tantric Magic, and on the history of Glastonbury, and
the Grail legends and am beginning, I think, to get at
least an inkling of what type of thing Dion Fortune
was involved in. Also, I think I understand what
Grant was driving at but I have a feeling he is slightly
off base for some reason but of course I have nothing
to support this feeling. That is, it seems true from Dion
Fortune's books that she "served Mary," that is that
she spent much of her energies exploring the
world/power represented by Binah on the Tree of Life
and Sakti in Tantric mysticism and the idea that this
"female" aspect of consciousness performs a kind of
kindling function for its opposite, the "male" aspect is
certainly expressed in her novels. But where or how
this all fits in I don't know and whether she "saw
herself as *the* magical shakti of the New Aeon," I know

even less. I don't even know what that means. I thought the "New Aeon" was Crowley's idea. I can't find much emphasis in Dion Fortune's books on a New Age or Aeon.

From *Aspects of Occultism*, p. 71:

"There are already portents of the Aquarian age . . ."

But:

"The work of the 5th Race, however, is far from finished and it will be long before the average man will function freely on the planes of Spirit. There is much talk about the 6th Race which talk is very premature." and really no feeling of messianic tendencies on her part. What I would really like to know is—what *did* Dion Fortune see herself as when she was "on her contacts"? Something more than what every woman can be? Or merely someone who was more conscious of her powers than others?

"Isis is the All-woman and all women are Isis." ("The Worship of Isis," p. 38, *Aspects of Occultism*)

There are some more things I'm confused about right now. First, was Dion Fortune in Stella Matutina or the Alpha et Omega, or both, possibly? According to Francis King, the name of the Outer Order of the Golden Dawn was changed from Golden Dawn to Alpha et Omega by an agreement of Mathers and Brodie-Innes sometime between 1908-1913 and according to both him and Kenneth Grant, the group which Dion Fortune first joined, in 1919, was an English Temple of the A.O. under Brodie-Innes. The London Temple that she changed to in 1920 under Mrs. Mathers and Mrs. Hayes would also have been called the A.O. at that time. No mention is made of Dion Fortune in reference to Stella Matutina until she had formed the Inner Light, at which time, as you mentioned, you were in close contact with them and they attended some of your rituals. And I take Stella Matutina to be the name of the rebel branch of the Golden Dawn formed by Dr. R. W. Felkin who broke allegiance with Mathers.

Also, was Dion Fortune actually Brodie-Innes' pupil or was she just "under" him in an official way since he was the leader of the branch of the Order which she at first joined?

Another thing is that I don't have a clear picture of the Glastonbury center. I understand that the Abbey ruins were bought by the Church of England and that Bligh Bond was made curator, that he was eventually dismissed by the trustees, that while he was there he created a stir with his archaeological investigations and that also a minor artistic revival occurred there at that time. But I don't understand Dion Fortune's references in *Avalon of the Heart* to "my guest house" (p. 106) and "the monastery itself became a guest-house of exceptional interest." (p. 74) And: "the 40 ft army hut," "a hostel for Avalonians." And "The British Israelites opened a centre in the house that was once occupied by Bligh Bond," etc.

Besides Kenneth Grant, I've also written to Israel Regardie who met Dion Fortune three times in 1933 and I have received a very nice letter from him but he doesn't seem to be able to remember too many details. I may be able to go with my husband on a business trip to California this spring and could question him further then. Mr. Regardie also said that Basil Wilby of Helios would be able to provide some information but when I wrote to Mr. Wilby, he said that he never knew Dion Fortune personally. *He* suggested I get in touch with a Mrs. Evelyn Heathfield who he says was with her in the "Land Army" in World War II and a Mrs. Helah Fox, but I haven't followed these two up as I thought that one of them might be the same woman you were trying to reach and I don't want to confuse things. Then, I wrote to Francis King but have heard nothing at all from him. Another person I was thinking would be good is Charles Richard Cammell who knew Mrs. Hayes very well but I don't know whether he is still alive or not. I should find out soon enough though because I wrote to him anyway.

Incidentally, the man I mentioned who has given me some guidance in my work, said to me that he thought that Dion Fortune had been a servant at one time, that she had been a maid or servant of some sort at that "educational establishment." Do you know if this is true?

Also, what about the periodical *Inner Light* which Dion Fortune issued herself? How many issues did it run? Do you know how I could get hold of any?

I don't suppose that a week in England will really be enough. It is all I can spare right now but I may be able in 1974 or 1975 to come for a longer period if I find it will be necessary.

Thank you also for the information about the Inner Light. I would like to include a history of the Inner Light—during and after Dion Fortune's time and including the two offshoots from the original— that is, if I can get enough information. Do you know anyone in either of those two groups who would talk to me?

That is all for now. I have heard your winters are mild compared to ours: I'm looking forward to our meeting.

Sincerely,

Janine

P.S. I have not received the copy of that article yet. I can easily xerox it and send it right back.

Cambridge, Massachusetts
November 17, 1973

Dear Mr. Butler,

Since I haven't heard from you I am assuming
the dates I suggested to you are satisfactory and have
made reservations to leave Boston on Friday, January
4th at 9 P.M. This flight arrives in London on Saturday,
January 5th at 8:15 in the morning. I would like to
stay in London that day and night and to come to
Southampton the next day (Sunday, the 6th). Please
let me know before the 21st of December whether this
time is really all right for you. I have not as yet
thought of a place to stay in Southampton and would
appreciate it if you could recommend one if it is not
too much trouble.

I will have to be back in London on Saturday,
January 12th for the 12 noon flight to Boston. That
should give me six full days. During that time I will be
able to see you anytime but I will leave the schedule of
meetings up to you as I don't want to tire you need-
lessly and can very easily find other things to do in the
inbetween times.

So I will be looking forward to hearing from you
soon. Thank you again for all your trouble.

Sincerely,

Janine

Cambridge, Massachusetts
November 18, 1973

Dear Mr. Grant:

Thank you for your letter of August 9th. I have
located the issue of *Man, Myth & Magic* in which your
article appeared—in the library at Llewellyn
Publications in St. Paul, Minnesota, and they are
sending me a xerox copy.

What you say about Dion Fortune gives me much
food for thought. The more I learn about her, the more
I realize that she was a very complicated human being
and that it will take me considerably more time to sort
the various levels of her personality.

I would like very much to have an opportunity to
ask you some more questions and to discuss certain
details of this matter more fully. I am planning to be in
England January 5-12. Most of this time I will be
spending with W. E. Butler and the people he has
arranged for me to meet who knew Dion Fortune but I
would like, if possible, to see you also. My plane
arrives in London on Saturday, January 5th at 8:15 in
the morning and I won't be going to Southampton
until the following day. If you have that Saturday free,
it would be the best time for me to meet with you.

Please let me know soon whether this arrange-
ment would be a convenient one for you.

Sincerely,

Janine Chapman

Mr. Grant replied that he would be very pleased to meet with me but said the date I had proposed was not at all convenient. He suggested three alternate dates: January 9, 10, or 11 at 11:00 A.M. He stated that there was very little he could tell me about Dion over and above what he had already written. But he added: "As far as concerns her work and details relative to the 93 Current with which she often identified herself, that is an entirely different matter and there is much that can be discussed."[4]

Mr. Butler wrote to say that he was arranging for me to meet Mrs. Evelyn Heathfield and Miss Helah Fox during the early part of the week. He said he would try to get Mrs. Christine Hartley and a Mr. Gough. Evelyn Heathfield had been a fellow student of Dion Fortune's at the agricultural college that turned out to be the establishment at which Dion had suffered her psychic attack. Helah Fox was an early member of the Fraternity of the Inner Light. Christine Hartley was a member in what may be termed the middle period of the fraternity. Mr. Gough was another Inner Light member from the same period. Mr. Butler repeated his warning that I would get no information from the Society of the Inner Light. He said, "They seem to want to forget Dion Fortune ever lived!" Mr. Butler said he hoped that he and I could get down to Glastonbury on Tuesday, January 8 to see the Tor, Chalice Orchard, Chalice Well, the abbey, and the grave of Dion Fortune, but he said it would depend on petrol rationing and other things.

---

[4] 93 Current is a term derived from Aleister Crowley's book *Liber 93 vel Nikh* in which he described his struggle to overcome his addiction to heroin. He was apparently successful in this effort until seven years before his death when his doctor prescribed it for him for his asthma. The word *NIKH*, the name of the Greek goddess of victory, adds up to 93 when you use a kabbalistic system of numerology. The number of Thelema (Greek θελημα) another term used by Crowley, meaning "will," also adds up to 93. The term "93 current" as used by Crowley's followers specifically refers to the tradition of sexual magic originating in ancient times, revived by Aleister Crowley, and accessible to all those who are able to tune in to this "channel."

On page 195 of *Aleister Crowley and the Hidden God*, Kenneth Grant states his belief that "the survival of the individual [in the new Aeon] will depend upon the degree to which he has assimilated and identified himself with the Thelemic Current, whether he happens to have heard of Crowley or not. This Current is characterized by elasticity, fluidity, an ability for spontaneous adaptation."

In his next letter Mr. Butler said that he had reserved a room for me for two nights at a place in Southampton where he usually booked his American friends. He said he would meet me at Southampton Railway Station on the 7th, we could have lunch together, and then go over to his place and "have a good talk." There was a final exchange of letters prior to my departure:

Cambridge, Mass. 02140
November 30, 1973

Dear Mr. Grant:

I have received your letter of November 24 and will try to meet with you on one of the dates you mention, for even though you only met Dion Fortune twice, there are some questions I think you could answer for me.

As soon as I know my schedule of meetings with W. E. Butler, and if there will be time available, I will let you know which day is best,

Sincerely,

Janine Chapman

Cambridge, Mass. 02140
December 19, 1973

Dear Mr. Butler,

Have received your letters 1 and 2. Thank you
for reserving a room for me. We have heard rumors
that BOAC may cancel its Boston-London flight after
Dec 21 through January but they have said they will
send me through New York or on another airline if
that happens.

Then—I was planning to get the 10:46 train from
Waterloo Station which arrives in Southampton at
12:14 but the last I have heard is that not all of your
trains are running. If that one is running, I'll be on it. If
not, I'll be on the soonest one after that and if all the
trains are out, I'll take a bus. I don't have any sched-
ules for the buses yet so I can't give you a time but will
try to let you know ahead if it seems I may have to
take one.

I do very much want to make the visit to
Glastonbury that you suggested and hope nothing will
prevent it.

I'll let you know immediately if I have to make
any last minute changes but will be sure to get there
one way or another.

Sincerely,

Janine Chapman

P.S. My married name is Mrs. Michael James. Chapman
is my maiden name and since I use both for different
reasons, it causes some confusion. Sorry.

19 Dec 73 e.v.

Dear Janine,

Do what thou wilt shall be the whole of the Law!

Thank you for yours of December 10. I am not on the telephone but unless I receive word to the contrary I shall look forward to seeing you on Friday, Jan. 11 at 11:00 A.M. The above address is a five minute walk from the Tube Station.
Love is the law, love under will.

Yours fraternally,

Kenneth

The last letter I received from Mr. Butler just prior to my departure, however, had some troubling news. He said the travel situation was in a very mixed condition, and he wondered whether it would really be wise for me to visit with him at this time. He said the train drivers, who were presently defying the government, were disrupting a great deal of rail traffic, particularly in the southwest part of the country. Should the fight between the rail union and the government get worse, he said, then the disruption would be worse.

Regarding our proposed trip to Glastonbury, he said that Glastonbury was very difficult to get to except by road. The railway that used to serve it had been torn up and the nearest rail station still running was Bath, which is quite a way from Glastonbury. The local buses run into Wells, and ordinarily we could have gotten a taxi from Wells to Glastonbury but with the petrol restrictions it was very doubtful if this would be possible. Renting a car would pose the same problem due to the petrol restrictions. "As Glastonbury is a key-point for any serious consideration of Dion Fortune's work, I am strongly of the opinion that we should do best to postpone a visit there until later in the year when, we hope, the traveling will be back to normal." In the event I did decide to come, he repeated that he would be at the Southampton Central Railway Station to wait for the train, plus the following one if I was not on the first. He gave me his telephone number and asked me to phone him between 7:00 and 8:00 P.M. on January 7. He ended with good wishes for the New Year.

I appreciated Mr. Butler's warnings about England's labor and energy crisis, but I did not want to postpone my trip. I was too far along in my preparations; I felt it was now or never, and whatever obstacles I would meet with over there I would just have to overcome.

Chapter 4

SETTING FOOT
ON ENGLISH SOIL

I flew from Logan Airport in Boston Friday evening, January 4, 1973, excited and nervous, full of expectation and apprehension. It was exhilarating to set foot the next morning on English soil. I felt instantly closer to Dion Fortune. I went by cab to my hotel, the Charles Dickens. They gave me a very comfortable room. It had a front view of a lovely English street with a row of townhouses and old-fashioned street lamps. I spread out my notebooks and research materials on the extra bed and planned my next move.

That night I telephoned Mr. Butler as he had instructed me to do. It was wonderful hearing his voice on the phone. He gave me Evelyn Heathfield's number so that I could arrange to meet with her. He said he was also hoping I could get in touch with Christine Hartley, author of *The Western Mystery Tradition*, who had been a pupil of Dion Fortune during the 30s and 40s. He told me she lived in London, and although he didn't have her telephone number, he was sure he had her address somewhere and would look for it. We arranged to meet the following Wednesday at the Southampton Railway Station. I then turned on the radio to hear the news on the economic situation. For some reason, all the political turmoil seemed foreign and irrelevant. It mustn't have worried me too much because I soon fell asleep.

The next day, I packed up and took a taxi to the Royal Court House, a less expensive hotel not far away on Gloucester Terrace. The room there was dreary. I felt a depression of spirits and a mounting anxiety about the grandiose goals I had set for myself for the remainder of the trip.

I received a call from Evelyn Heathfield early on Sunday evening. Her voice was warm and friendly, which lifted my spirits considerably and made me feel renewed optimism. Again I was having a conversation with someone who knew Dion Fortune! We made arrangements to get together on Tuesday morning. She said she was looking forward to meeting me.

I spent Monday in London shopping and sightseeing. I didn't want to miss the British Museum but it took so long for me to walk there along what seemed an endless Oxford Street. At last I reached Museum Street in Bloomsbury where I turned to the right. Here was an array of bookshops and antique shops, an atmosphere of learning and of history preserved. Then I was on shady Russell Street where I saw the grand portico of the museum behind iron railings.

It was 3:30 P.M. when I went through the revolving doors into the museum's large high-ceilinged entrance hall. Although my guidebook said the closing time was five o'clock, a sign as I came in said the museum would be closing that day at four due to the energy crisis. I had only thirty minutes to sample the riches of the museum's vast collection!

I walked to the left of the entrance door and found myself among an impressive display of Egyptian antiquities. From there I walked into ancient Assyria, Babylon, and Persia, and finally to ancient Greece and Rome. It was exciting to think that Violet Firth must have visited these or similar exhibits, fertilizing her youthful imagination with images from classical mythology and dreams of possible past lives. The opening chapter of her novel, *The Winged Bull*, came to mind where Ted Murchison found retreat inside the museum and communed with the human-headed bull that had guarded the temples of Nineveh.

I was primarily interested, however, in the pre-Christian British artifacts. My search was soon satisfied by a splendid display of British coinage found on the first floor. The exhibit was fascinating, and I wished I had more time to enjoy it.

By 4:00 P.M. when the museum was closing, my feet were killing me. I didn't realize that another short walk north would have brought me to London University where Violet studied the new psychologies of her day and to Tavistock Square where, in the Theosophical Society Library, she read the book *The Ancient Wisdom*, which stimulated her encounter with the masters of occult philosophy.

I dreaded the long walk home, so I summoned up my courage to try the underground, the British subway system. This turned out to be an experience in itself, especially since it was the middle of rush hour. The underground seemed more crowded and hectic than the subway in New York City, if that could be possible.

When I got back to my hotel, I decided to see if I could get in touch with Christine Hartley. I looked in the phone book and found one Christine Hartley listed. I called the number. The woman who answered said that this Christine Hartley was dead and, in any case, she had not been Christine Hartley, the author. She said she got a lot of phone calls for the Christine Hartley I was seeking and had found out that she had been a literary agent. She suggested that I write a letter to her in care of her publishers.

I didn't have time to write and wait for a response; I only had enough money to stay in England a week. I felt that Miss Hartley was somewhere there in London. Her book *The Western Mystery Tradition* was published by Thorson's. I called them and explained my situation. They told me they could not give me her address or telephone number but they could forward a letter to her for me. They said that if I sent a note right away they would send it right on to her. Perhaps there would be sufficient time for her to respond. I immediately wrote a note to Miss Hartley, giving her the address and phone number of my hotel.

Chapter 5

EVELYN HEATHFIELD AND HELAH FOX: MEMORIES OF DION FORTUNE

The next day (Tuesday, January 8th), I went to the railway station and took the train to Lewes in Sussex. It was an exciting ride, watching the English countryside go by and observing the people on the train.

At Lewes, I took a taxi from the train station to Paddock Studios, where Evelyn Heathfield lived with her husband's brother and his wife, Mr. and Mrs. Heathfield.

Evelyn Heathfield lived and worked in a large artist's studio with a bed-sitting room adjacent to the house. It was a pleasant, simply decorated, sunny room. The easel, the clutter of canvases and paintbrushes, and the smell of oil paint made it obvious that Evelyn Heathfield, although elderly, was very much an active artist. There was also a large desk and a chartreuse bookcase decorated with yin-yang designs under a painting on the wall. On one of the bookshelves was a framed photograph of Dion Fortune.

Evelyn Heathfield was a large woman, stout, with short, straight gray hair. She was an imposing figure, an outspoken woman of strong opinions, with a keen sense of humor. I remember thinking she looked "arty" like an old Greenwich Village woman. She had trouble walking and was slightly hard of hearing but was very enjoyable company. She was wearing a purple and green dress with a scarab brooch, and was in a festive mood because I had arrived on her 81st birthday. First we had tea with sandwiches and fruitcake. Later we drank sherry, and afterward we ate a vegetarian "meat loaf" made from chestnuts. It was delicious. With it we had a salad and rice with which we drank black currant juice.

Evelyn Heathfield turned out to be the person who solved the mystery of where Dion Fortune experienced her famous psychic attack. Mrs. Heathfield had met Dion Fortune when she was still Violet Firth, when both of them were students at Studley Agricultural College in Warwickshire. She was able to tell me many details of their time there. Mrs. Heathfield's account, as well as my subsequent research, confirmed that Violet's psychic attack did in fact occur at Studley and that it was Dr. Lillias Hamilton, the Warden of Studley, who attacked Violet psychically, precipitating a nervous breakdown. I drew this conclusion in spite of the fact that Evelyn Heathfield had a strong reluctance to acknowledge Dr. Hamilton as "the Warden" described in *Psychic Self-Defense*. Her reasons for concealing the facts were undoubtedly the same as Dion Fortune's. They both wanted to protect the reputation of Studley and that of the warden.

What follows is a transcript of the tape recording I made of my visit with Mrs. Heathfield. Shortly after I arrived, Mrs. Heathfield made a telephone call to a friend of hers, a medium by the name of Hope Todd, and that is where the tape recording begins.

E. Heathfield: Thank you. Oh dear. Well, now listen. We've got here a lady from America called Mrs. James. Did I tell you? Well, she's here by appointment through Ernest Butler. She is hoping to write a biography of Dion Fortune and we're trying to unmuddle things that nobody seems to be able to get clear, and the question is—and I think I've told you about it—when did Dion Fortune go through her very difficult experience of being hypnotized and finally done in and then went into the country to recover? I have always said that that happened before she went to Studley. Well, I know that Ernest Butler thinks it was Studley—that place—and so much fits in I've begun to waver, but I still do not believe it was. Would it be possible for you to get in touch with Dion Fortune and ask her about that sort of thing? Ask her if she would tell you. Was it at Studley or was it before? Yes, whether it was the warden of Studley who reduced her to the pulp she said she did. I don't believe so. She has said since to me, through you, that she had several nasty experiences before she went to Studley. And I've always taken it for granted. But on the other hand, you see, it does fit because I do know that Mary Peers was very much under the warden's thumb, or everybody thought she was. It all fits and there was a person called Auntie Barclay. Yes, a funny old thing that we all called "Auntie" and—no, no, she was a student, a mentally deficient student, you see, that Vi mentions in her description of the educational establishment where she broke down. But I'd say so dead certain that she never broke down at Studley; she just stayed there a year and then went. I'm sure it wasn't. Yet it's all so muddled. Could you—Yes . . . well, that's what I've always thought—it was *because* of that that she went to Studley. Yes . . . Yes . . . But I feel that when she wrote her book, as writers and authors will do, that she almost intentionally sort of muddled the places up. But it could be that I'm . . . but I still feel so certain it wasn't and however much I hated her, I respected the warden and I . . . I . . . I just absolutely refuse to believe that she was capable of doing that. But then I begin to doubt. Well, will you see if you could find out. Oh, you know just as soon as you like. I can get Mrs. James' address and write to her. She's over in this country for inside of a week. Just a week, you see, she's just arrived and she's going down to old Butler tomorrow, and I don't quite know about her movements afterwards. She's sitting beside me here. Yes. Yes. Yes. It happened at Studley. What? Oh, you can? Oh, well. All right thanks most awfully. Ah, well, when will you do it? Will you really? Oh, marvelous. Well, if I ring you up again before the end of the afternoon and ask you? That would be marvelous. Thanks awfully my dear. How are you? My dear, 81, you can forget it, you can forget it. Yes we had a lovely party last year and I had quite a good time this year, too. But there is a letter from me in the post for you. Yes. Yes. Only a short one. Righto. I'll ring up later in the afternoon. Well, she's only here for the day. Helah Fox is coming over this afternoon and you know she's dependent on trains, when and if they run. All right, I'll ring up about teatime. Okay? Righto. Thanks most awfully my dear. That's great. She said she could distinctly hear Dion Fortune's voice saying, "My God, no it wasn't the warden!"

Chapman: Then it wasn't?

E. Heathfield: It wasn't, no. But she will. She'll have a session and see if she can get it through.

Chapman: It's hard to believe she would have said that about that person unless she felt no one would ever care to find out.

E. Heathfield: I'm quite sure she never would. But there you are. She's as good as denied it now.

Chapman: Well, thanks very much.

E. Heathfield: If I ring her up this afternoon, she'll have got it through.

Chapman: OK.

E. Heathfield: It'll be rather fun.

Chapman: Yes, that will be.

E. Heathfield: I'm glad I'm right. Dr. Hamilton was absolutely straight; I've always thought so. But it didn't . . . But then, we shall know. Now what can I offer you to eat? Fruit? Have a pear?

Chapman: A pear would be nice.

E. Heathfield: Have you got Mr. Butler's *How To Develop Clairvoyance* and *How To Read the Aura*? Because if it's not in this one, it's in one of those two little ones. [Evelyn Heathfield's sister-in-law entered at this point.] Come and talk. Or listen to us talk.

Mrs. Heathfield: All right.

Chapman: It was very good. I've never had a meat loaf that wasn't made out of meat. It was good.

Mrs. Heathfield: Yes! We haven't had it before. I'm sorry to sort of try something out on you.

Chapman: It might be in this. Do you have *How To Read the Aura*?

E. Heathfield: No.

Chapman: OK, well then, if it's in that one I can't find it but if it's in this one I will. Can you tell me something about the course of study that you took there in the college? What was it that you were studying? And how were the classes arranged?

E. Heathfield: We were studying horticulture—or agriculture. I was in the horticultural branch. We went out to practical work every morning and came in for a lecture from about a quarter past twelve until one—most days. Then we'd go out to practical work again from two till half past four. After that it was, you know, study or do what we liked.

Chapman: And what did the practical work consist of?

E. Heathfield: Well, gardening.

Chapman: So, then in a sense you were a lot on your own. Were you given any directions?

E. Heathfield: Oh yes, we were under the head gardener, under professional gardeners, men gardeners, you see. And did what we were told. It was a huge market garden with a large number of market houses and plant houses and open land.

Chapman: So you were growing vegetables?

E. Heathfield: Yes. Everything to do with gardening: vegetables, and in the market houses it was oh, carnations, tomatoes, cucumbers, everything. It's difficult to say—like any ordinary market garden.

Chapman: And the things that you grew would actually then be sold?

E. Heathfield: Oh yes, they certainly were.

Chapman: How many years did people usually spend there?

E. Heathfield: Two years. People who were really going to work as gardeners afterwards spent two years or three years. I was there two years.

Chapman: So most of the people that were there were actually training to go someplace afterwards and be a gardener?

E. Heathfield: Yes, most of the younger ones were. Quite a lot of them.

Chapman: And were they all women?

E. Heathfield: Yes.

Chapman: I see. I always thought that men were gardeners.

E. Heathfield: Ah, yes they were and they are. But that was the very early days of women beginning to be gardeners. A lot of them went into market gardening and ran their own market gardens.

Chapman: And what was your reason for going there?

E. Heathfield: Because my mother wanted me too, that's all! Because I couldn't be an artist. She frowned upon having a daughter as an artist. She said daughters have done a little painting always, and she wanted us to do something that had never been done before.

Chapman: But you gave it up after two years?

E. Heathfield: Well, the training was finished.

Chapman: But you never used it?

E. Heathfield: Yes, I had a job. For the next six years I had jobs. And then the first war broke out and I had various jobs. In actual fact the job that I was in for the war was for a lady who was extremely interested in the occult. And she had a medium friend. And it was there that I learned first about the occult and occultism. It was there that I was first woken up to it. And after that, the war was over and I came home. I actually trained after that as a garden designer. I worked as a landscape gardener on my own for years. And then as things go, I don't know, they sort of fizzled out. And the Second World War came and I was caught up in all the various relief work in the town. Dion Fortune apparently used what she learned there that year because she was in the Land Army during the war.

Chapman: What did they do in the Land Army?

E. Heathfield: They went out and took men's places on farms and in gardens. But it was a nationally organized thing. They either joined the forces in the Women's Army Corps or the Women's Naval Corps. So while the men went out to the war, the women took their places on the farms.

Chapman: And she did this after she left this training school?

E. Heathfield: As far as I know. I think she has stated in one of her books that she did work on the land for a short time. But she obviously gave that up, and then she went and worked with Dr. Moriarty.

Chapman: But also in almost all of her novels, she expressed a love of gardening. It's either the heroine or the hero who likes to grow things and whichever one it is, she is projecting herself into that character, you feel.

E. Heathfield: No, I doubt if that's the one she projects herself into because she didn't like gardening.

Chapman: She didn't like it?

E. Heathfield: No, she didn't like it. She's said to me since, through Hope Todd, she has said to me that, "You didn't like gardening; neither did I, but it was the beginning of our career."

Chapman: Isn't that funny? Because I always thought that she did. And if she didn't, it must have been just that she had been around people who did and so she wrote about them.

E. Heathfield: Yes. But you see, she was writing all the time. And I gather from her novels a side of her was that she was very interested in food, good food and feeding. In all her novels somebody is given to food. You know in *Moon Magic* Lilith Le Fay was always turning out some sort of—

Chapman: But if we can't tell from her novels whether—she had some people in her novels who like gardening. She also has people who are interested in cooking. Well, if we're wrong about one, maybe we're wrong about the other. She did write that book about the soybean, but—

E. Heathfield: I've never heard of that. I only know that she was there for health reasons only and she has actually said to me—I might search. I've got the whole book there, communications from Vi and from my husband. But she did actually say once, "You didn't like gardening; neither did I. But it was there that you got your contact with the Earth Mother," which I have been very strongly contacted with all my life.

Chapman: Well, she apparently was, too.

E. Heathfield: But she was with the Moon, Isis. She was very keen on the Moon and Moon magic and the Moon and the priestesses of the Moon. Whenever she mentions priestess of the Moon, that is herself, I'm quite sure.

Chapman: It's difficult to tell from her books. She's piecing together a lot of different people and a lot of different ideas. It's very difficult to pick out her own personality from the books. Even if you have a feeling, you're not sure whether it's really accurate.

E. Heathfield: She was a good novelist and was able to project herself into anything. I think. I don't think she could help it. But I had it straight from the horse's mouth, she did not like gardening, thank you very much. But she did it because she had to. And it didn't do her any harm. She was very glad to have had it, I think. I suppose when war broke out, the first war it was, women turned to anything that they could, and she'd had this training, a year of it anyway, and she put it to good use and went onto the land again. I don't think it was the Land Army, because I don't think the Land Army was formed. There was talk about the Land Army, but I think she probably went and worked in somebody's garden, I don't know. But she also got out of it again as soon as she could.

Chapman: Yes, she does express a love of nature in her books, but most of the action takes place indoors. The characters are always cooking a lot and also, they seem to be interested in environments, creating interesting and pleasant environments.

E. Heathfield: Oh, yes. Helah will tell you about this when she comes. She ought to be here soon. Dion had a house—3 Queensborough Terrace in London. She did marry, you know. She was married at the time and then they parted. And she went on with the place. But I gather the whole of Queensborough Terrace— she lived, I suppose after he left her, I don't know—in one base-ment flat, basement room herself. And the rest was used for different levels of initiateship, you see. Helah will know that because she was part of it all. She was a full initiate.

Chapman: She had this place in London, and she also had a center at Glastonbury?

E. Heathfield: Yes. You've read—what's that book about Glastonbury?

Chapman: *Avalon of the Heart*?

E. Heathfield: Yes.

Chapman: Yes, that's really a lovely book.

E. Heathfield: It's a lovely book, beautiful book.

Chapman: She's also very evasive in that book. She doesn't say anything definite about herself or about her group, nothing defi-nite, just little references here and there.

E. Heathfield: No, she does keep herself in the background, absolutely and completely, and has no use for people who didn't do that. She was very keen about that.

Chapman: This is one of the things that has always impressed me about her—she was not an ostentatious person, and she wasn't too crazy, if you know what I mean. To study something that is as obscure as the Kabbalah, it's difficult not to become unbalanced.

E. Heathfield: Oh, yes. And that's why so many people fail, because they lose balance and they use the powers that they gain, they use them for wrong purposes. They use them for their own gain and not for love of their neighbor. And she's very strong about that.

Chapman: Yes, she is. It's also a problem when you're studying something that so few people study, it's difficult to know how to integrate your own personal life into the rest of the world. I think a lot of other occultists have not been able to do that well. It's not an easy task. That is one of the things that impressed me about her, that she was able to do this.

E. Heathfield: Live in the world and yet out of it.

Chapman: Yes, she was. She was able, it seems to me, to do that successfully.

E. Heathfield: She quite certainly was. She was supremely successful.

Chapman: She chose something that was very good—psycho-analysis. It was a good bridge between the two. It was accepted. Not as much as nowadays but—

E. Heathfield: It was accepted, yes.

Chapman: After the end of the First World War, psychoanalysis attained quite a vogue in England. It was very popular. Do you remember anything about that time?

E. Heathfield: After the first war or after the second war?

Chapman: After the First World War.

E. Heathfield: No, I don't remember much about psychoanalysis then. You see, I was the daughter of a perfectly conventional doctor and I didn't come across it very much. When did I first hear of psychoanalysis? I suppose—was it between the wars? No. I needed it myself in between the wars! Yes, I suppose it was when I was working with Olive Pixley. It was the very beginning of the second war. But now it's a household word almost. I don't know about in America, but here there's a terrific upsurge of interest in what people used to call spooky things, occult things.

Chapman: You mean right now?

E. Heathfield: Yes, right now, a tremendous lot—groups growing up all over the place, following all sorts of paths, the Sufis and there's radionics and there's this and that and the other—all hating each other like poison.

Chapman: Each one thinks that they are the one.

E. Heathfield: But she [Dion] was always, and always is—I mean whenever she writes to me now she says, "Everybody must find their own path and follow it, and all paths lead to the same thing if you do rightly."

Chapman: Yes, she always said that. She never said that—

E. Heathfield: She never said this is the only way. Never.

Chapman: No. And she never said that she knew everything about a certain thing. She often mentioned that there was a lot yet to be found about these things and we could never be sure. No, I think she was very objective, relatively speaking.

E. Heathfield: Oh, yes. Oh, she was. And she knew a lot of different things. She's always saying to me now, "Let people choose their own path." And when I first went to Olive, all the time I was with her—I hoped to be a healer—and then when I started the Helios training, I always thought I should turn out to be a healer.

And it was a long, long, long time before I realized that everybody is a healer if you didn't worry about being *a healer*. If you are following a path, you give out something that somebody else can take.

I, well, I thought of this, that, and the other but, you see, I always wanted to be an artist. My husband and I worked together, and he had the scheme of starting the Rural Arts School so that people coming back to normal life after the last war would turn to the arts. And he was right. He started it and the County Council took it up and helped him start the classes and paid him a salary for doing it. And we started with one class in 1944-1945, I suppose it was, two classes in villages near her. And when he retired in 1963— he was 70—we had got over a hundred classes going all over the county. We weren't teaching them all, but they started the classes in all the villages all over Sussex. They had art groups and, well, he had to retire at 70 and he gradually failed and all my spare time was taken up to looking after him, until he went, when I was absolutely devastated because I always took for granted that my life's work was to hold the other end for him, and when he went I should go, too. But, not a bit of it. I had to stay. It's only in the last year that I have started up the classes here again. And that is what I have got to do—paint, paint. And that is the final painting! [Mrs. Heathfield indicated a large oil painting of the Tree of Life hanging in the studio.]

In the midst of our discussion, Miss Helah Fox joined us. Miss Fox had known Dion Fortune from the 30s until her death and had been an inner member of the Inner Light Fraternity. She had lived both at Chalice Orchard and at 3 Queensborough Terrace. She was with Dion Fortune the day Penry Evans left and was present at the first Fortune-Crowley encounter. She was a cultivated, refined woman of approximately 50 years of age, with a trim figure and a very fine speaking voice. She was conservatively dressed, and I remember she wore a camel-colored sweater. Her mind was very clear and her memories vivid. She stated that she was still on good terms with the present day Inner Light members.

Fox: And several of us went along there [3 Queensborough Terrace] and lived there and she, despite everything, she got that into the shape she wanted it. And she had a friend whose name I can't remember now. She was just a personal friend. She painted all round the lower floor, scenes from the Book of Death, you know, the Egyptian scenes from *The Egyptian Book of the Dead*. They were fascinating. I was only thinking of this some time back, wondering what happened when the premises were taken over by somebody else, and what they thought of them! Because it was very vivid.

E. Heathfield: It doesn't still exist, Queensborough Terrace?

Fox: Oh, yes. It does. Because they remained on after. When she died, they remained there for quite awhile.

E. Heathfield: May I ask you a question? I'm anxious to know things, too. In the original house, where was the temple? And were there different layers of initiateship on each floor?

Fox: Well, the temple was on the middle floor of the house and the floors above that were used for living quarters. And below was the library. We had a very good library and an office. And there was a very good addition on the building, which was useful in many ways. Then when this bomb fell, it was a question of not being on the premises at all, but it blasted away the back of the house. And though we went back into number 3 about 1941, we couldn't use the back addition at all. And that made a good deal of difference. But the temple remained intact to the end.

Chapman: When did the bomb drop?

E. Heathfield: I think it must have been October, 1941.

Chapman: And then did you try to move back there?

Fox: She never moved back into it. She continued to live in 21.

Chapman: She moved out of 3 Queensborough Terrace when the bomb dropped?

Fox: Yes, it had to be. The whole place had to be vacated, you see.

Chapman: And she moved into 21 Queensborough Terrace, the same street, and then she stayed there and then the rest of you moved back into the—

Fox: Yes, but there was always somebody living there with her.

Chapman: I see.

Fox: There had to be, because she couldn't live there without someone to answer the door and generally protect her when necessary.

Chapman: Now, Mr. Butler said that she died of leukemia. You were there?

Fox: No, I wasn't. I had gone back to my ordinary work.

Chapman: Do you have any idea when she found out that she had leukemia?

Fox: That was one of the very early cases of leukemia, and I don't think it was suspected until really it was too late to do anything. It was at the time that the "box" was just beginning to be known. One of our fraternity did learn about the "box" and was using it. And was terribly upset because DF wouldn't listen about it. She said, oh no, this was not for her and would never use it.

E. Heathfield: Do you mean the radionic people?

Fox: Yes.

E. Heathfield: Oh, she knew about that, did she?

Fox: Well, she was told about it. Whether she did anything at all I don't know. I imagine that she didn't because when the news came that she was seriously ill, this particular friend got in touch with me. She says, "It needn't have happened! It needn't have happened! It needn't have happened, if she would only have listened."

Chapman: Why? What does it do?

E. Heathfield: Who was the man who did it? Let's give her his name. Yes, Delvaux, that's it. He discovered that by using a box—but then they used it by touch, didn't they? First of all, they touched. All the time as they made the inquiries.

Fox: Yes, they had knobs in it, nine knobs, and they dialed, tuned it in. You had to have a specimen of the person concerned. Either a hair or a drop of blood or something. And you could diagnose and, more than that, you could also treat. It's developed further than that now and a great many people who first of all learned to do that found that they didn't need the intervention of the box at all, you see. It was all to do with the development, which is very, very interesting but rather difficult to trace out, of all the different psychologies through that period. From the early 1920s until after the War. And it was about, I should say 1944—1943 or 1944— that she became interested in Jung. And then she went to consult the best Jung practitioner who there was in London. That was Mrs. Tony Sussman. And she went and talked things over with her and she sent a number of her students to her.

Chapman: She didn't hear about Jung until 1943?

Fox: Oh, she must have heard of Jung quite a lot but she wasn't interested. She began to read and to recommend other people to his work, you see. But it didn't coincide entirely, didn't fulfill entirely what she wanted. No psychologies had done because really and truly she knew without having it all rationalized a good deal more than any of them, you see. And so though she went to Mrs. Sussman for a while, she decided that it wasn't what she wanted, and she gave it up. But quite a number of her students, as I did, went on with the field of psychology.

Chapman: Are there still psychiatrists who practice Jungian analysis?

Fox: Oh, yes. It's developed quite well and in America, too, surely.

Chapman: There are so many different types of psychologies nowadays.

Fox: Yes, I can't remember the name of the first man who went out there.

Chapman: Now, tell me what brought you into the Inner Light.

Fox: Well, one is always seeking for something in this world. Something more, you see. I had been trained as a teacher of older children, older students, and I was very anxious to get more. I happened to have met someone who knew her and she said, "Well, why not take her course?" Which I did.

Chapman: So you were a teacher?

Fox: And I returned to that. I didn't give it up at all, completely. My whole interest and way of life went back into that after her death. I didn't go on with Initiate work at all.

Chapman: So really, your main involvement in the occult was during this period when you knew Dion Fortune and when you were in the Inner Light? And since then you have lost contact with the Inner Light?

Fox: No, I'm sorry, I must correct. I'm still on very good terms with the Inner Light. I correspond with various members, and I know how they come and, in some cases, how they go. After all, I had some very close friends among them, you see.

Chapman: Do you mind if I use a tape recorder? I should have asked you before.

Fox: No.

Chapman: OK, so now I'm getting the idea of what I should know then, what this period did for you in your life. Although you left it, it must have left an impression on you.

Fox: Yes, I continued to use the material they had furnished me. And I taught Qabalah whenever they wanted to be taught Qabalah. That was my part of it, you see. Some people did more on the mystic side, some people did more on the nature side, and some people took the occult.

Chapman: You were in this now for ten years?

Fox: Yes.

Chapman: Could you give me some idea, as much as you would want to do, of 3 Queensborough Terrace? I have a picture of the physical location, but I don't have much of an idea of what the training was like, how it was structured.

Fox: Well, in the first instance they had these correspondence courses which led on to the study of the Tree of Life, of which she had written the book. There were the two books, really and truly, which at first were not printed. And for a long while the *Cosmic Doctrine* was not put into print at all. The *Cosmic Doctrine* took in everything. And the Qabalah, the Tree of Life—she only dealt with the ten spheres of the Tree of Life in her book. Have you read it?

Chapman: Yes.

Fox: She published that and there were a number of courses which people followed. But at that time most of the study was achieved through meditation. Students were taught to concentrate and meditate very well indeed.

Chapman: The people that were taking the correspondence course?

Fox: Yes. She had arranged a number of teachers and they were themselves passed into the initiate group. They undertook the training of the students and so the recognition of anyone who was really fit to go on. If they were doing really well in their studies, and they passed several courses, they would be invited to an interview. A great many people didn't meet her at all until that interview. And she would have others with her. One would act as the secretary. Some people would be sent back to do the same course more than once. Some people just fizzled out, you see.

Chapman: Now if they passed the interview, then what?

Fox: Well, then it was a question of whether they could be initiated, whether they wanted to be initiated. Not all of them did.

Chapman: Now, if they did, and if it was judged that they would be able to, would they come and live there?

Fox: Oh, no. No, that wasn't possible. There was very limited accommodation really. How many did we have? About six or eight. I happened to go because of the war, you see. When the war broke out, I was evacuated, and my mother, too. Then a question arose, of course, and we had that year that they called the phony war. By that time a great many children had come back to London. And so I came back to London to teach, and I was offered accommodation in Queensborough Terrace. So it all came about in that way, you see.

Chapman: Yes, I see. There were only about six or seven people living there. And the other people would come there.

Fox: Yes, some people traveled a great distance. Some people came all the way from Devon each time to a meeting.

Chapman: What about those who were accepted for initiation? How was their training structured?

Fox: Well, if you were going on, you continued. You got many books to study, you had reading lists, you had to keep your meditation. It was as much a rule almost as much as a monastic life would be. Part of the time, at any rate.

Chapman: I've heard that she was very good at making the course of instruction fit the student.

Fox: Yes, she was. She was very good at that.

Chapman: I've also heard that she went too far sometimes, that she interfered with some of her students' private lives.

Fox: Well, it's very difficult to say, really, that she did too much. After all, the beginning of the study gave people as a tenet that nothing ever happened by accident. Nothing can happen by accident. Therefore, anyone who is as advanced as she was may not be doing it consciously with that end in view, but as a channel for that sort of thing. And it provided tests which had to be passed. I know that some people felt very badly about being rejected. But of course the rejection was quite as much from within the person as it was from without.

Chapman: You mean that if they were rejected that meant there was something in them that didn't want to be accepted?

Fox: Yes, that they didn't want to be accepted, really truly.

Chapman: I see. Yet it is true that she could have made some mistakes.

Fox: So does everybody in all walks of life. Personally, I am of the opinion that such things, though they may appear as mistakes, judged as behavior, have a purpose in people whom they reach. I think that's happening around us all the time.

Chapman: I guess it's like saying it's all for the best.

Fox: No, I'm not saying that it's all for the best, in that sense. But I have seen things which appear to be quite from our standard the opposite of what was to be wished doing just the right thing for that person.

Chapman: I understand now.

E. Heathfield: Was it her saying, "He that never makes a mistake never makes anything"?

Fox: I don't remember that it was actually hers.

E. Heathfield: I think she's quoted it somewhere.

Chapman: So you don't feel that her influence or her guidelines were too strict for you?

Fox: The training that she gave me and several others was really of the utmost value to us. It made the difficult period of adjusting to life after the war much more possible. Of course, I had also the great benefit of the Jungian studies as well.

Chapman: So you had study, you had readings, and you had meditation. Did you have an initiation ceremony at a certain point?

Fox: Oh, yes. They were held in the temple.

Chapman: Were they on the Golden Dawn system?

Fox: Well, I don't know what the actual details of the Golden Dawn was. I imagine that all of them, all occult schools, follow that same pattern. There has to be a temple. There will be a ceremony and a ritual which is drawn up and rules are made thereon and it goes on like that. I suppose the easiest example is that of Freemasonry. They go through the various grades. They can hold office in lodge and so forth. They meet a regular number of times each year and so on.

Chapman: Well, she had come originally from the Golden Dawn. And originally the Inner Light was set up as part of the Golden Dawn. So I was wondering if they used the Golden Dawn system of grades and initiation.

Fox: I can't answer that because I don't know. I don't know what the Golden Dawn system was in detail. It seems to me obvious that it must have been on that. We had at one time many grades. But as I say, that sort of thing is common to all occult schools, you see. But each school, each teacher, will provide what they find necessary for that particular way which they're working.

Chapman: And she must have changed things and made up her own ways of doing things.

Fox: Yes. Actually, it was done, I should say, as a team. She always had someone to work actually opposite to her, and a number of people round about her as well. And assisting in meditation would be done. And she herself, of course, was a very good medium. She would get instruction. And that's how things went.

Chapman: At this time was she working with her husband?

Fox: Yes, he did work in the actual grades.

Chapman: What about this man Mr. Butler has spoken of, Loveday?

Fox: Yes, Thomas Loveday.

Chapman: Did you know him?

Fox: Very well.

Chapman: Could you tell me something about him?

Fox: Well, he was a musician, a very fine musician, indeed. And he understood the significance in that respect of music and its relationship with number, rhythm. And he had always been particularly in charge of the mystical side.

Chapman: What do you mean by that?

Fox: Well, the mystical side was definitely Christian. It was run very much along the lines of church services. I think that was one of its greatest points. And during the worst phase of the war that was continued. You could go every Sunday and meet and meditate. We did a great deal of meditation. For the protection of our homeland.

Chapman: These were generally under the direction of Loveday?

Fox: Oh, yes.

Chapman: What kind of person was he?

Fox: He was a very gentle, quiet sort of person, warm, a loving man. He had really the relationship of a father in God to a great number of people who came.

Chapman: Was he older than Dion Fortune?

Fox: Yes, he was older. And about the time that she fell ill, he began to develop the symptoms of Parkinson's disease. The last years of his life were very much crowded by that because he could not attempt the things which he wanted to do. He could no longer play in the temple because of the shake and so on.

Chapman: What instruments did he play?

Fox: The violin and the cello, I believe. All of the things were destroyed in the hall that was blitzed—near to where BBC is now.

E. Heathfield: Queen's Hall.

Fox: That's right. He wasn't there but his instruments were.

Chapman: I'm also interested in finding out about Dion Fortune's relationship with her husband. I've heard that her marriage was unhappy. Yet you say that they worked together in the Inner Light.

Fox: Yes, they certainly did. I shouldn't say that it was unhappy. It went through a number of phases, so she herself gave me to understand, until somewhere—I think it should be the end of 1943. I'm not good at the dates because I didn't write them down. I remember that I came home to the flat in the afternoon and there was a note saying, "I want to speak with you when you come in," and I went down to talk with her. She said, "Well, the time has come, and Merl has left. And that's the end," she says. "I feel it will be a shock to some people to know that this happened, but it's just like a leaf withering and falling off."

Chapman: What did she call him?

Fox: She always called him Merl. He was not an easy personality. He didn't fit in at all well with the close kind of relationship that we had during the war. A number of them found him difficult. He was a doctor. He was a Welshman. He had the most remarkable speaking voice and a very kind personality, very suited to do what she gave him to do, which was to work on the side of the green ray. But there it is, it just ended and he disappeared out of her life and out of ours.

Chapman: Sometimes the woman in a marriage is more fully developed as a personality and the husband doesn't like this. Could there have been something like this going on?

Fox: Well, I think there was a certain amount of that quite possibly. He did have a very good free hand, all the same.

E. Heathfield: Isn't it true that very, very, very few men can live the life of being second fiddle to the wife?

Fox: It's very, very difficult for the positive one. But you see, he was a specialist in his own field, and he had a consultation room and that sort of thing. And it seemed likely to work well because of that. He became head of the health department for Reading, Officer of Health, is it?

E. Heathfield: And an out-and-out Celt!

Fox: He was.

E. Heathfield: Married to an out-and-out Nordic.

Fox: Yes.

E. Heathfield: Too difficult.

Chapman: You said that she gave him direction. Was he under her?

Fox: There was no one who was on her level. At any time. From time to time there were difficulties of that nature. There was more than one man who felt that he should be sharing the throne. But they couldn't. It wasn't simply that she made it apparent that they couldn't. It was what they, inwardly, I think, knew.

Chapman: They couldn't because they—

Fox: They were not of that grade.

Chapman: That she was?

Fox: Mm.

Chapman: And this was something that was understood in an unspoken way by everybody?

Fox: I don't know that you could go as far as that. But I mean we did know that a great part of the life of the community came into it through her work. As I say, she was the medium. At that time there was no other medium in the group at all. That changed afterward. They had to change because she was practically withdrawn.

Chapman: When people realized that she was going to be gone, what happened?

Fox: I wasn't living with them at that time. But very gradually there was fear that the different parts were being taken over. The man who had worked so much with her, and was about her age, for a brief time managed affairs, but only for a very brief period. Then it was handed on to someone who was selected to be Warden and is still Warden.

E. Heathfield: How long before she went into hospital did she know that she'd got leukemia?

Fox: I don't know.

Chapman: I've heard that things in the Inner Light have changed a great deal and that they don't want to have any association with her name or with her in general. Is this true?

Fox: I think it is, to a certain degree, true. It's arisen because certain people there are really very afraid of the personalty cult. There were times when she was criticized in the group, itself, quite freely. And I can quite realize how it came about that they decided. Though I thought that it was in itself a confession of inadequacy. You see what I mean?

Chapman: Not exactly, Why wouldn't they want to honor her memory?

Fox: Well, they do owe the whole thing—a very large amount of it—to her as the agent through whom God expressed certain things. But now they have definitely cut out as much of it as they could possibly do.

Chapman: And this is for spiritual reasons?

Fox: No, I wouldn't think it was spiritual. I think it was really psychological reasons. Psychologically, they have quite a lot of lost points, you see.

E. Heathfield: Do you think it's possible they fear that the same thing would happen to her as happened with the Secret Doctrine woman—that started Theosophy—

Fox: Oh, yes, Mme. Blavatsky.

E. Heathfield: Blavatsky. Well, there are people now who if you say anything to them, they won't accept it if they can't find it in Mme. Blavatsky's *Secret Doctrine*. And, oh yes, you can't have that because it's not there. Well, things have got to go on. Things have got to go on.

Fox: Yes.

E. Heathfield: I'll tell you what we have done this afternoon. We started sort of discussing and the eternal question came up—when did she have that experience at the educational establishment that she was so ill afterwards? Lots of people—and even Butler—have said to me, "Well, that must have been when she was at Studley. It must have been the Warden at Studley." And there is extraordinary similarity. They both had Wardens who had been in India. Both knew things. And they both had a slightly low-mentality lady there as a student who everybody called Auntie. And people have said to me, even Mrs. James said to me, "She got that from there. It's the same place. That was where she had her breakdown." And I still swear that I'm dead certain it was not. I'm sure it was not, and yet it's so alike. So we rang up Hope Todd.

Fox: Oh, yes.

E. Heathfield: And I said, "Can you, Hope—I told her what we were doing—can you contact her and get all the information you can this afternoon? Because I should like to know. And she said, "Oh, I can tell you. She's shouting it in my ear now. 'It was not! My God it wasn't!'" she said. So we shall hear. I'm going to ring her up again later. We shall hear if Dion Fortune has got anything she wants to say on this subject.

Fox: Yes.

Chapman: In all of her books she was very evasive about her life.

Fox: I think she offered her life—and it was a very full life—as a channel. The earthly trappings of it are really not very important. Yes, it's very interesting and if you were starting to study her books, it would be interesting to have an outline [of her life]. But I don't think it's going to go on to a biography, with that point of view. I'm being very frank with you.

Chapman: I understand. But it seems to me that the story of her life would be valuable as an example or lesson to others, especially to other women. Many young people are growing up confused and are looking for role models and spiritual guidance. There are two or three biographies of Aleister Crowley available right now. I'd hate to see his life story become more of a formative influence on today's young people than the story of Dion Fortune.

Fox: I agree with all that. Quite.

E. Heathfield: But since you've been here I've begun to realize how extremely difficult it is going to be to get enough definite things to make a biography of her.

Fox: You see she hadn't got any [one person] with her all the time. Her life is divided up into very definite sections and intervals. At one time Mr. Butler had a great deal of time with her. He understands her very thoroughly. Each of us in turn had that, you see. You see, Glastonbury held a very, very great place in her life and ours. Glastonbury was a sanctuary to which we went. She set up her home there on the side of the Tor, and I always felt she was at her very best at Glastonbury, and so was Mr. Loveday.

Chapman: You were there, in Glastonbury?

Fox: Oh, yes. I went to Glastonbury at Easter time. That was the great rallying time. Although before the war—I must have gone to Glastonbury in 1937, I should think. And even during the war I spent some time there.

Chapman: Now, this was at the same time that you were undergoing training at 3 Queensborough Terrace?

Fox: Yes.

Chapman: How did she manage these two places?

Fox: She had someone there [at Glastonbury] who was living there all the time with a housekeeper. People went down for a weekend or for holidays and for certain times, particularly, as I say, at Easter and Whitsun, Corpus Christi, we went down and stayed there as a group. We had a sort of sanctuary where we could meet for the meditation. It had its symbols. We used the water from the holy well and lived a communal life. Music had a great part in it. People came and stayed there with us who had a contribution to make but who didn't belong actually to the group. There were some very interesting contacts of that sort.

[At this point, the tape ran out. During the short time it took to turn the tape over, Miss Fox and Evelyn Heathfield continued talking so that a short amount of conversation is missing.]

Fox: But she said that was the sort of thing that happened. I think she was really very wary about psychology for that reason—that people at that time thought it could do everything and that you hadn't got to start at the bottom and work up several or down several levels. Jungian psychology appealed to her very greatly, so much so that at one time I think she may have even thought, "I will go out and meet him when there's a chance." And then she thought, "No, you can't put all your weight into one thing. You know quite well that isn't sufficient." But you see the fact that she married a doctor—she was working through the whole [all the levels] all the time. That was the important thing.

E. Heathfield: And whoever was there, connected with her, had to be with her for a time.

Fox: Yes!

E. Heathfield: And when it was over, he just went.

Fox: Quite. Quite.

E. Heathfield: Was she terribly upset by it or had she known it was got to happen?

Fox: She knew it had got to happen. I think she had been upset over the idea of it.

[Long blank in tape]

Fox: Loveday had had an experience while staying at Glastonbury. At that time there was a group around Alice Buckton. Alice Buckton lived—the house is still in existence—it's still there. And she had the idea of gathering a group of artists around her. *The Immortal Hour* was produced there and there were potters and carvers and various people. And I think that originally Dion Fortune and Mr. Loveday went to stay at the house and got to know Alice Buckton. But of course their two personalities were not going to be very long compatible together. And unless you did what Alice wanted, I gather you were very soon out. And they went to stay at a cottage further along the road, and they had a remarkable experience. So when the opportunity occurred to get this piece of ground, which was quite considerable—it's been divided up now—they took it over. And Mr. Loveday said we could get some of the army huts that were being offered after the First World War. And he himself did a great deal of that work. He was very active. They set up a largish hut, which served as a common room. There was a kitchen and three bedrooms to it. And then they put others along. And it was a remarkable place, really.

E. Heathfield: Where was it actually? Exactly where was it?

Fox: On the foot of the Tor. You have to walk up beside that property to get onto the National Trust land.

E. Heathfield: Oh.

Fox: And it was a good size.

E. Heathfield: Was it sort of on the opposite side of the road to Chalice Well?

Fox: Well, yes. The lane goes up that goes round the Tor. The well is on that side. The water used to come out and flow down in the brook beside the roadway because during that second war we had a man who was the trapping officer for that part of the country, and he used to come over and come in. He was a particular friend of mine. He would come in to stay and have a meal with us and so on. And he always used to say, "Wash it down with the holy well water!" [Laughter] Well, Dion Fortune had her own hut eventually put up, which was very pleasant. And she would stay there and sometimes people would come and stay with her as well. Actually, I think it was—it must have been somewhere about 1936—my mother went down to stay there while they were there.

Chapman: There weren't any regulations against putting up these huts?

Fox: No. You had to have an application. I mean, it happened all over the place, didn't it? You saw people put up the most peculiar sort of buildings. In those days you could do it. No, it was very well done. Mr. Loveday knew what he was doing. He organized it.

Chapman: What were these huts made out of?

Fox: Well, they had been made of timber, I suppose, and they had brick foundations. And then the hut was erected on these. It was wood and I think a kind of paneling that was largely asbestos. It was well-roofed. I think Mr. Shelley lives in the big one now to this day. John Shelley lives in the big one.

Chapman: Somebody still lives in one of these?

Fox: Yes. He's [John Shelley] very interested in all this, the nature side of it particularly. He believes that there's water that flows down through the Tor which is even more sacred than that from the well. I don't hold by that at all. I don't think that Dion Fortune did. Water is water. But we had some wonderful times there. And of course the Tor is a very strange and mysterious formation.

E. Heathfield: Yes.

Chapman: I'm going down there to Glastonbury on Thursday.

Fox: Oh, are you? Where are you going to stay?

Chapman: I don't know yet. Mr. Butler knows some people there that I could stay with. Mr. Butler was going to drive us, but he doesn't seem to feel as if he's well enough to go.

E. Heathfield: He's very bad on his legs. And when you got there, he would find it awfully difficult to get around.

Chapman: Yes, that's probably what he's afraid of. But tell me more about the inside of these huts. I'm trying to get a picture of them. What did they look like inside?

Fox: Well, they were very comfortably furnished, as they had to be if they were going to be comfortable for her. She believed in that sort of thing. All the rooms had beds that could be folded up, you know, against the wall. Either they would go up from the bottom that way or they would go sideways up to the wall. We had a very fine long refectory table that could sit about sixteen people, with long forms that were padded but had no backs. Some people didn't like that and they were always juggling to get a seat at the two ends. We had a lovely open brick hearth on which we burned peat all the time. The scent of the peat was marvelous. One of the members did the cooking for us, and we had very nice meals. There was a very large veranda, oh, as wide as this room is, all along one side of it, looking down so that you looked not up at the Tor but down. And the garden was well planted. They all had a hand in that. Of course under direction from the one who knew. She had just a marvelous show in the springtime with the apple trees in bloom and all the bulbs up.

I remember once we were there for Easter, and we went into the chapel, oh, after breakfast, I forget what time. I suppose it would be about half past nine. We were some time in there, in meditation and so on, and when we came out there had been a snowstorm and the pollen hills were all white and all these beautiful flowers were all covered as if with a cloak. It was most marvelous! You couldn't forget it. And yet it all disappeared by the time we sat down for lunch. We were back in the spring again.

Chapman: Mrs. Heathfield has said that Dion Fortune didn't really like gardening. What do you feel about that?

Fox: Well, I never saw her do much gardening [Laughter]. She did some.

E. Heathfield: I've got it definitely. "You did not like gardening; neither did I."

Fox: I can well believe that. But she liked the results.

E. Heathfield: Oh, yes. She wanted the results. I like the results if somebody else will get them.

Fox: Various people did do quite a lot of that.

E. Heathfield: Would it be, do you think, a good thing to give Miss Chapman this thing by Bernard Bromage to read? I always find it interesting. I know Ernest doesn't like it. He said he's not fair to her. But I read it through again and I can't see where he's not fair to her. I think it's extremely interesting.

Fox: Well, he [Bromage] came and went a lot during that particular time. And I think he did get to know her. From the point of view of an outsider, actually, a journalist.

E. Heathfield: But I think he brings out her absolute calmness and her courage during the air raids and that sort of thing. Would you like to take that with you? I can find my copy for you.

Chapman: Yes, thank you. And I know I'll have a lot of questions after I've listened to all the tapes. Could I write to you and ask you them?

Fox: Yes, do.

E. Heathfield: Yes, give us your address in America. We mustn't lose touch now.

Chapman: Okay, that's good. So, now I'll just keep on asking questions until you're too tired to answer them [Laughter]. So, you would go down to Glastonbury then on these special occasions or for certain periods of time. It was like a vacation place. Most of the time you were working in London.

Fox: Yes. I was working.

Chapman: And this closely knit group of people was around her at that time. About how many were there in this inner group?

Fox: Well, as a general rule there must have been at least eight people at that time. And we changed over. I mean it's surprising when one looks back. I meet some of them now and they say,

"Well, you know in the time when I was living with so and so."
You see, we didn't stay on for years and years. We moved. Mr.
Loveday was always there and Dragon—what was her name? It's
awful, I always think of her as Dragon.

E. Heathfield: Now, when you had a group of eight like that working one of those very intense things, did they all have their feet
firmly on the ground or was it apt to get a bit—

Fox: Oh, no! [Laughter] Awesome things happened! Awesome
things happened! But the thing you must somehow get hold of is
the feel of her. She was, at that time in particular, so intensely alive.
And she was really quite beautiful because of this inner thing. And
life was fun, too. Even though Merl went off and it seemed as
though we were maddening at times. She would say, "Well, I must
have a whipping boy!" [Laughter] And she would. "There must
be someone who was responsible for such-and-such a thing." And
she would take it out on them. In that respect she was almost like
a military person. But it was quite exciting to go out anywhere
with her and see what would happen. Of course, during the war
we kept in contact with a great many different groups, all of whom,
like ourselves, were really working by thought and meditation
and prayer to protect Britain from invasion.

E. Heathfield: Yes.

Fox: And we did a great deal not only of meditation but also working at the images, building them up, particularly the archangelic
images.

E. Heathfield: Yes.

Fox: And occasionally things happened there. Several times we
had bombs outside 21 Queensborough Terrace, but they didn't do
any damage to 21. That was the interesting part about it. It could
cause a good bit of disturbance on other planes, and we had to go
off for a rest. I had by that time, you see, got my mother in
Northampton, so I could always flee there for a weekend if things
were very bad. I remember I came back once from Northampton

and someone had been sent to meet me at the station and missed me. And so I came down into Queensborough Terrace and found everything shattered. It was really rather a state. During that time, as I say, she used to speak to a group on Sunday mornings. And on that particular occasion when things were so bad, she said, "Well, I'm going to Norfolk." We had some friends there. "And I'll be away for at least five days. I must have rest to get over things." And so they said, "What about such and such?" "Oh, well," she said, "so-and-so can take it." To the great consternation of so-and-so. Then she said, "That's all right. You know perfectly well that we'll get through." And I do think she did very often during that time do by telepathy what would have been too much strain for her physically.

E. Heathfield: It's a curious thing, it's funny, that the girl I remember as Firth is the woman I know now as Dion Fortune. I still only think of her in a sax apron and gardening uniform. And her sense of fun.

Fox: Oh, yes.

E. Heathfield: And wild practical joking.

Fox: In some ways—I mean during that time of the war—she was deeply moved emotionally. I remember coming back from Northampton when Coventry had just been bombed and having her about. I had something, a letter that I think a young serving officer had written. I read it aloud and to my astonishment—the only time I ever saw her moved to tears—but she was. She was very much alive on all four levels.

Chapman: Did she maintain the same general structure of the group, when you would go to Glastonbury? That is, was she in charge?

Fox: No, as a general rule, if we went to Glastonbury, and she happened to be there, she was there on holiday. She was "off" so to speak. She might state, "Well, come down tonight and we'll talk over what's to be done." But as far as the pattern of life was concerned, whether there would be assembly in the sanctuary or not, that would be up to Mr. Loveday because Mr. Loveday—really, at Glastonbury—acted as a priest.

Chapman: So she didn't lecture at Glastonbury?

Fox: No, she only lectured in London.

Chapman: What about the correspondence courses? Was she in charge of those?

Fox: Yes, but she didn't answer them. She didn't do the correspondence course at all after I knew her. That had been given out. She had several people. I myself did quite a bit of correcting. And she wouldn't allow the teachers to be known personally to the students. You didn't know who was correcting your work. Sometimes it worked out into the most amusing situations. Someone would say, "My teacher says I'm not to do so and so and I can't do that. Or, I am to do so and so and I must do it," and you happened to be talking to the person who *was* your teacher but you didn't know, you see.

Chapman: When you took the correspondence course, did you take it through her?

Fox: Was it she who corrected my work? A man who had been in the army, a retired colonel, was responsible for a lot of my training, as I learned much later on . No, I think she knew very little about me as a person until I was called up for an interview. I saw her with Dr. Evans and Mr. Loveday and they asked me various questions of what I thought of various things.

Chapman: Could you tell me something more about the interview?

Fox: Well, I was just trying to remember what it was that Dr. Evans said. Oh, that he was sometimes sorrier for the germs than for the patient. And I stood up about it. Apparently not many people dared differ from Dr. Evans, and it amused him very much.

Hope Todd's Channeled Session

Received by Hope Todd, Tuesday, January 8, 1974, at 2:15 P.M.

We greet you.

Vi here Evelyn. Thanks for your help. Your memory is good! *Studley*. I was sent there after trying to cope with a number of psychic experiences which were disturbing because I did not understand them completely. My family became alarmed and then frightened for my sanity. True the Warden was told of this, in confidence, when I arrived at Studley. Her efforts to try to dissuade me from progressing along the Path, were strong and tedious. She confused me for a while and then my future became clear to me. I HAD TO GO ON. And so I left Studley and continued with my chosen work on the Path. It was a testing time and I was often reduced to what you so aptly call pulp. I admit that many situations after my time at Studley reduced me to pulp, for a while, but Studley was the turning point. It was my "Garden of Gethsemane." You and Mary P. were, without realizing it, at the time, my positive Angels. I see it all so clearly NOW. Thank you for your help. I did have many powerful experiences at Studley and these finally made up my mind for me as to which Path I should follow.

The old gardener Bob once said to me, as we were working in the garden, "Follow your own star." I never forgot this advice.

Love to you all
Vi

E. Heathfield: Miss Chapman, do you know shorthand?

Chapman: No.

E. Heathfield: It's only that I hope to get on to Hope again. If she's got a long message.

Chapman: Well, we can put the tape recorder up to the phone. That should pick it up.

E. Heathfield: From the phone? Oh, right! You be ready! I'll ring through again now to her.

Chapman: OK.

E. Heathfield: All right with you?

Fox: Yes, yes.

E. Heathfield: Hello, my dear. Any message? Well, look we've got a tape recorder here that Mrs. James says will pick up from the phone. Can you then make it out? Hang on a minute! Yes, we'll tell you when it will start. You put it against this, do you? OK!

At this point, I put the tape recorder up to the phone, hoping to catch the spirit message on the tape. However, when I got back home (to the USA) and replayed the tape, the part of the tape where the spirit message was supposed to be was completely inaudible. I was very disappointed. I wrote to Evelyn Heathfield and told her that the spirit message didn't pick up. She wrote back, sending me Hope Todd's handwritten copy of the message. [The channeled session appears on page 98.]

A very curious thing happened when I was going over the editor's queries on the manuscript for this book. In order to answer the editor's questions, I had to replay most of the tapes. At the point where I had put the tape recorder up to the phone, the spirit message came out very clearly in Hope Todd's voice! This was, of course, quite a startling experience for me, for I had played the tape countless times before with the same tape recorder without getting a bit of the spirit message at all.

E. Heathfield: You reach out behind you and get that little notebook off the desk there and I'll get you to write down your address.

Fox: I think it was very interesting. She had such a marvelous power of words. She would come and give a lecture. And I'm not talking about just a private lecture in London. She went and gave a lecture in Hawkins Street at which I was present, and there were a number of different societies that had heard she was going to speak and went to hear her. And she came and stood on that platform without a note. And she hardly moved. She looked at the people and she just spoke. I can't think actually what the lecture was about now. But she never hesitated. But once. And that was when she realized that Aleister Crowley was in the audience. And he definitely was there to get across at her if he could, you see. And then she finished. She came down and spoke to the people who'd organized it. And he thrust through and spoke to her, and he attempted to make her take a book. He said, "I would like you to read this." And she said, "Not just now." And she managed to escape without it. She said a more determined attempt to make a link with her, she'd never known. But she really was marvelous the way that she would speak and the way in which really and truly she made us speak. Because I did quite a lot of speaking at one occasion or other and always I felt, "Oh, it'll come." And it did. In fact, I've never since been able to either talk to a class or anything else from notes, and I think that is largely due to the fact that we were so trained to concentrate.

Chapman: Colin Wilson claimed, in his book, *The Occult*, that Dion Fortune was a student of Aleister Crowley at one time. But Mr. Butler was very quick to point out to me that that wasn't true at all. Even when I read it it seemed to me to be incredible, that she could never have been his student considering his attitude toward women and how independent she was of authority. But what you said right now sounds so believable and right. Of course, they were living at the same time, and they knew of each other and perhaps he was a little bit resentful of her status, especially because she was a woman and he liked always to put women down.

Fox: Oh, yes, he always wanted to dominate over women. That's all they were to him, just something for him to sharpen his claws upon. [Laughter] But she had, of course, remarkable poise and remarkable presence.

Mrs. Heathfield: It's been an interesting afternoon!

Chapman: Oh, yes. You know, I've heard that she did correspond with Crowley, that there were some letters between them. Kenneth Grant mentioned that to me.

Mrs. Heathfield: Milk?

Chapman: No, just the tea is fine. Kenneth Grant mentioned in his book, *The Magical Revival*, that he had seen a stack of letters between her and Crowley and that they were on their way to Crowley's legatee in New York and that he didn't believe that they ever reached there.

Fox: I think that after that occasion he did write to her. Whether she really did answer in person, I doubt. I think it's much more likely that she got the secretary to say what she wanted to. I certainly don't think that there was a stack of correspondence between them. She was far too much aware. Thank you so much.

Mrs. Heathfield: Do you take sugar?

Fox: No, thank you.

Mrs. Heathfield: Do you take sugar?

Chapman: No, thanks. It's very good tea.

Mrs. Heathfield: It's only Indian, in case somebody didn't like it. I was tempted to make something unusual, but then I've come unstuck with some of my visitors so I thought I'd play safe.

Chapman: Her other papers, do you know what happened to them? Do you think that perhaps they're in the custody of the Inner Light?

Fox: I think they would be, yes.

E. Heathfield: Are you going to fly down to Ernest or are you going by train?

Chapman: No, I'm going to go by train there and then get a car to go to Glastonbury. Mr. Butler said that the best way to get to Glastonbury from Southampton is by car. Anything else is too complicated. And so I'll do that. I'll get the car in Southampton and after I figure out how to drive it, I'll take it up there.

E. Heathfield: His little house is absolutely impossible to find, isn't it?

Fox: Very difficult.

E. Heathfield: Did you see Trafalgar Square at all?

Chapman: I don't know. What is that?

E. Heathfield: The big square in London with the Nelson column. It's in Trafalgar Square that you see the Norwegian Christmas Tree which can only be lit for a little while. They bring this beautiful tree every year to us in remembrance from the wartime.

Chapman: I'll have to look for it. Is it near Oxford Street?

E. Heathfield: No, not very. It's between Charing Cross and Piccadilly Circus.

Chapman: Hopefully, I can go back there on Saturday. I'd like to do a little shopping before I go back. Another person that Mr. Butler is trying to get in contact with is Christine Hartley. Apparently she lives in London.

There was more casual conversation, but it was beginning to get dark, so I drew the interview to a close. After I said goodbye to Mrs. Heathfield and Miss Fox, Mr. Heathfield drove me to the train station. I took the train back to London feeling very happy. I had finally made contact with Dion Fortune. (Later I was to discover that January 8, 1974, was the 28th anniversary of Dion Fortune's death.) Confirmation of the theory that Studley College was where Violet Firth underwent her psychic attack was to come after I got back to the United States. I will speak more of that later.

Chapter 6

Ernest Butler and the Real Secrets of Dr. Taverner

The next day, which was a Wednesday, I was up early again to catch the train from London to Southampton, which is a very old seaport settlement dating back to the Norman occupation. In the Middle Ages it traded in French wine and English cloth. The town really began to expand when it opened its docks in 1836, and again in 1872, when the railway gained access to the waterfront. Today it is a terminal port for transatlantic passenger traffic. It is also an important British cargo port.

Mr. Butler met me, as promised, at the Southampton Central Railway Station. He was of medium height, maybe 5'6" or 5'7". He was wearing a gray overcoat under the top of which was visible a clerical collar and under the bottom a pair of carefully creased trousers. He wore a fedora of soft gray felt and was using a cane of polished wood with a crooked handle. He had the very pale white skin of the Celt, a round face, thin lips, and a kindly smile. Behind a pair of wire-rimmed spectacles were clear blue eyes, intelligent and alive with an other-worldly vitality.

I will never forget that meeting. There was a paternal sort of goodness about him that made me warm to him instantly. Besides this, I felt an odd sensation as if I had finally come home, as if I had known him all my life but had been separated from him for a long time. As he clasped my hand, I felt an invisible outpouring of love. I knew for the first time in my life the true power and efficacy of a white magician.

We took a bus to another section of the city. Mr. Butler asked if I would like to eat before we continued on our journey. I agreed and we entered a nearby restaurant. It was not a fancy place—more like a cafeteria or family diner. He ordered kidney pie and I asked for an omelet. Our order came swiftly. We ate in a comfortable silence. After a while he did ask me how I liked my omelet, and I said it was fine. Back then I was not at all good at small talk and could think of little to say except the questions I had prepared for our interview later. Observing him from up close, I realized how old and frail he was. I knew that he had been fighting pneumonia and bronchitis over the past year. It was obvious to me that he was making an extraordinary effort.

After our meal, we took a cab to the guest house in Southampton where he had booked me a room. He waited in the cab while I dropped off my suitcase with the proprietress, a congenial woman who was also a friend of his. From there we went to his house, which was a long ride out into the country. "House" is not the right word, though, because it wasn't a house. It was a large 500-year-old Tudor cottage made of limestone with a thatched roof and casement windows of glass crisscrossed with lead. To someone from the United States like myself, it seemed ancient, or out of some fairy tale.

I was overcome by the age and magic of the place—on the outside with its gigantic oak tree and on the inside where he showed me a working fireplace as old as the house itself. But once inside, when I saw how old-fashioned the interior of the cottage really was, I began to have doubts about the operation of my tape recorder. Mr. Butler didn't think it would work, although he said he didn't object to being taped. I told him I had an adapter, a device which would allow the recorder to work with the English electrical system, but he appeared not to know what I was talking about.

He showed me into the front room on one side of the house. The old walls, the crude mantelpiece adorned with pieces of old crockery and knickknacks, the windows with diamond-shaped panes looking out on the bleak winter countryside, and especially the ethereal quiet over the whole place seemed to take me back much further than Tudor times, almost to pre-Christian Britain itself. I felt as if I'd flown in a spaceship instead of a mere airplane, and as if I'd traveled more in time than in distance. And young and eager as I was, I sat down beside the old seer and listened to his story.

I did have trouble with the tape recorder. Mr. Butler shook his head as if to say he didn't think I'd get it to go. I was worried because I don't take shorthand. I could never get down every word of what he would say. But at last the adapter worked and the tape started.

I can still hear Ernest Butler's voice today with its quaint Yorkshire accent just as he spoke to me then in the failing afternoon sun at Little Thatches, Hillstreet, Calmore, Southampton, England. (See figure 2, p. 108 for a photograph of Little Thatches.) I now share Mr. Butler's words with you.

Butler: . . . and I went down to Glastonbury. In those days—in the old days—there was a railway there, Somerset and Dorset Night Railway it was called. When I get to a place, I always find out when there's a train back. It sounds daft but it isn't so daft because you know how much time you've got and everything like that. So he said, "Half past six, sir." I said, "Right, good," and away I went. Well, I met Dion Fortune in Glastonbury and she told me about the origin of her group that she had at the time. She was linked up with a lady—oh, I'll remember her name presently. She was concerned with a kind of Glastonbury Renaissance, with art and music, Rutland Boulton, with *The Immortal Hour*, and other things like that.

Chapman: Alice Buckton?

Butler: Uh? Alice Buckton, that's right, yes. [Pause] All right.

Chapman: OK, go ahead now. That's fine.

Butler: Right. And so she told me that she was linked up with Alice Buckton and with all that kind of work and at the same [time] she was in link with Bligh Bond. I don't know if you've ever heard of Bligh Bond, have you?

Chapman: Yes.

Butler: Well, Bligh Bond was a very curious individual. I liked him, but he was a man who very easily made enemies. And he made an enemy of the dean of Wells Cathedral, who happened to be one of the big Anglican people concerned with the Glastonbury Abbey. Well, Bligh Bond at that time was doing excavations for the Somerset Archaeological Society in Glastonbury Abbey under the permission of the dean of Wells, but he fell foul of this man. Bligh

Figure 2. Little Thatches.

Bond was a grammar school boy and the dean of Wells was a lofty one from Cambridge or somewhere thereabouts. And Bligh Bond had a chip on his shoulder with regard to that and so he fell foul of him. It was rather unfortunate.

However, having met Dion Fortune there, I decided to join her group because it was definitely just the thing I wanted. I returned to London but I kept in correspondence with Dion Fortune and went through what was then their study course. And then in 1929 I left the service and I went to London to work. And I came to the conclusion that I might as well now definitely work with Dion Fortune's group—with the Inner Light. They had a center at 3 Queensborough Terrace, Bayswater, and it was there that I took my initiation into the Fraternity of the Inner Light and that was that.

Well, in the four years in between, I was dodging about all over the place one way and the other, and it was very difficult to keep touch. But I did keep touch and then, let's see, I finally joined in 1929. I finally became initiated into the fraternity. Well, now—ah, yes, I have the photograph here which I wanted to show you. And if you care to have a copy, I'll have it taken for you and you can use it which way you'll like, if you want to print it or anything like that. No, no, here we are, yes. There is one which was not included in the Society of the Inner Light incinerator business.[1] You can see Dion Fortune there with a band on her hair. Can you see clearly?

Chapman: Yes, I can see fine. It looks as if it was taken about the same time as that other photograph.

Butler: Now, I can tell you some of those people there. Her husband is there—the gentleman in plus fours there, Dr. Penry Evans— that's Dion Fortune, and this is her right-hand man, Mr. Loveday, C. T. Loveday. He was an official in the London Tramway Department. He was the man who was responsible for buying Chalice Orchard and the building on it, and also for getting the headquarters in London. He sold some of his own property and bought these places, you see. So he was the man who was really the right-hand man to all Dion Fortune did. And this lady, who died last year, she was Miss Lapbury. She was the most efficient secretary you could ever wish for. We called her Dragon. That was her name. We all had pet names.

Chapman: Yes, Miss Fox mentioned that, but she couldn't remember her real name. She could only remember "Dragon."

Butler: Yes, that's right. Well, there was A. B. O., as we called him, or His Nibs, Mr. Loveday. And that was Miss Lapbury. She was Dragon. Dion Fortune was Ferdy, and Dr. Evans was Merlin. His name was Merlin. Now this was the group around them. All of them have passed over now, every one of them.

Chapman: You say Loveday provided most of the funds?

Butler: Yes, he provided the funds, yes. Yes, he did. He was an official in the London Tramways Department. And he had some private means, too. He sold some of his property, which had been

---

[1] Mr. Butler is referring to the destruction of Dion Fortune's personal papers by Inner Light members just after her death. Unfortunately, Mr. Butler never had the chance to have a copy of this photograph made.

left him by his father, and with the proceeds he managed to launch the place in London and down at Glastonbury. He got the apple orchard. That's all it was, an overgrown apple orchard. He got it for practically nothing because nobody wanted it, you see. I wouldn't like to tell you how much—well, it's Mrs. King who's got the place now—what she paid for it is nobody's business, believe you me. But prices have gone up, of course. The price of land has gone up. A house which I had over on the other side of Southampton which I sold, has now been sold again and it's brought ten times what I got for it. Ten times! Same house. Houses around here are absolutely premium. You can get any price you like. Put a chicken hut up, you would get a couple of thousand on it, you know, that's the kind of thing.

Chapman: I know. Well, that's because there's not much land left.

Butler: Exactly, yes. Well, there you are. And if you'd like a copy of that for an illustration or anything like that, I'll print it for you, OK?

Chapman: OK, good.

Butler: Well, that's how I came in contact with Dion Fortune. But of course I had been doing occult work for years before that. I started my first experience when I was about 9. After that I had a continual contact with the psychic and the occult. And in 1915 I came in contact with a man who taught me most of what I know after Dion Fortune, a man called Robert King. He took me in hand and I was his pupil—well, until he died actually. I never let go of Robert King, not even when I was working with Dion Fortune. He knew Dion Fortune. They were the same kind of occult surroundings so that it didn't make any odds. But he was my first teacher. I think I've got his photograph here. He was one of the original bishops in the Liberal Catholic Church of which I'm a priest. And he was a great man. He was a very fine clairvoyant and clairaudient.

Chapman: What is the Liberal Catholic Church?

Butler: Well, it's all over the place. There's one in Southampton, of which I'm a member. Oh, by the way. You've heard of Carl Seymour, have you, by any chance?

Chapman: No.

Butler: Well, Carl Seymour was one of Dion Fortune's right-hand men. Again, a very fine chap. Old Gareth Knight in New Dimensions is running a series of articles by Seymour. They're pinched from the *Inner Light* magazine. Anyway, there's Colonel Seymour there. And the lady with the cat is my wife. The cat was Dion Fortune's cat down there. And that's just by the side of Chalice Orchard, that is. They're standing there where they used to sit and meditate in the mornings in the summer.

Chapman: How long was this magazine issued for, the *Inner Light* magazine?

Butler: The *Inner Light?* Oh, there were thirteen volumes issued, actually. You can get them through John Hall. He sometimes has a spare lot in. They're expensive. There's Robert King, my own teacher. My first teacher. A great man.

Chapman: He knew Dion Fortune, but he wasn't in her group?

Butler: Oh, yes, he knew her very well. There's a place which I hope you'll visit tomorrow. I took a group of people down to Chalice Well and I was explaining to them there all the bits and pieces.

Chapman: Who was this Seymour?

Butler: Colonel Seymour? He was in the War office as a matter of fact. He was a very fine occultist and a very fine speaker. And a good writer, too.

Chapman: Was he in her group at the same time that Loveday was?

Butler: Oh, yes. Yes. He's not on that lot though. He came in later. He wasn't in the original group. But Loveday was with her until she died. Well, he died after her, as a matter of fact. She died in 1946 and he died in 1947.

Chapman: Loveday was a musician, wasn't he?

Butler: He was. A very fine musician, too. Who told you that, by the way?

Chapman: Miss Fox.

Butler: Oh, did she? Oh, yes. He was a lovely musician. And a lovely man, too. If ever there was a real Christian walking about on two legs, that was A. B. O. Golly, yes! If I got half as good as he was I should do very well. He was really a good man in the right sense of the term. Ah, yes! My wife and I were in a sticky position because of the unemployment in this country. There were two-and-a-half-million people out of work, and I was out for two-and-a-half years. Not any work. Not nice. But Dion Fortune and Loveday came to the rescue and helped us very, very well. Materially and in every way. So that I owe a very great debt of gratitude to them both. On the purely mundane plane, let alone anything else. But Loveday was a lovely man. He really was. The only thing, he insisted on having a crystal set. He had no use for an ordinary radio set. Not at all. It must be a crystal set. Do you know why?

Chapman: No.

Butler: The purity of tone of the reception on a crystal is far better than any bulb reception.

Chapman: What did you get on the radio in those days?

Butler: Well, it was really called 2LO. "2LO calling," they used to say. There was one station used to be doing most of the broadcasting, and I've made many a crystal set up. It was fun, getting my cat's whiskers and getting it sorted out. And when you'd got it, it was good, if you had very good earphones. And A. B. O. did get a pair of good ones. He swore that it was the best reproduction of the music that he could get, and when someone offered him a bulb for sale he wouldn't have it.

Chapman: So his ear was very fine?

Butler: Yes, it was, yes. Nice chap A. B. O. Now, he was attracted to Dion Fortune in a very interesting way. He was in the Royal Flying Corps, which was, in the First World War, a precursor of the Royal Air Force. He was in the Royal Flying Corps, and he and a friend of his had just had a bit of leave coming. They'd just been discharged from the service after the war and his friend said, "Have you ever been to Glastonbury?" And Loveday said, "No." "Well," he said, "it's worth going down to see." So he said, "I'll run you down on my bike, if you like." So he got on back of this chap's motorbike and they came down to Glastonbury. That would be, what, 1923 or thereabouts. And, oh yes, a lovely place was Glastonbury. And this friend said, "Yes, we'll go up to the top." He said, "There's a lot going on here at a place called Chalice Well." "And," he said, "there's quite a lot going on. You might be interested in it. There's musical stuff. There's Rutland Boulton and all the rest of them. There's plays, amateur plays." A. B. O. says, "Oh, that's just what I want." So he went into the big yard at the back of Chalice Well. Chalice Well in the front was a school. It was a training college for Roman Catholic ordinants to the priesthood. They trained them there before they ordained them and sent them on foreign missions. But anyway, they left there and Miss Buckton had it then. So, in went A. B. O. in one corner of the courtyard at the back, and Dion Fortune came out at the other side. And they met in the moonlight. And she took a look at him and he took a look at her and that was that. And from that moment onwards he was her right-hand man for everything that she did.

Yes. A very nice chap was old A. B. O. He's buried next door to Dion Fortune in Glastonbury cemetery. If you can get there tomorrow, I'll give you a few sketch maps. I'll draw a little bit, and you can see where you are. It's not very far out from Glastonbury. Thank God the geography at Glastonbury is fairly simple, and I've drawn it so many times for different people that I know it by heart.

Now, that was taken at my friend's place. I'll give you a letter of introduction to him. That was taken at midsummer last year. We got permission from the Church of England to celebrate our Liberal Catholic Communion in St. Patrick's Chapel in the Abbey. And that was a very great privilege because, of course, the Anglicans have hold of the Abbey and they're not very fond of letting anybody else do anything. But they had opened this chapel for what they call other denominations, provided you can prove that you're respectable. And we got—by a bit of luck—we got permission to celebrate. So I went down and some of my pupils came down, some of my students and supervisors and all the rest from the course. And we went down there and well, it was a glorious scramble, I'll tell you. Originally, when our priest at Glastonbury wrote up, he said, "They'll be about a dozen of us there. Just a little family affair." I said, "Oh, yes." And then I told one or two of my supervisors and they told some of their students, and the word had got round by a grapevine elsewhere, and when we got down there that chapel was crammed, actually crammed, over fifty people lodged into it. At the utmost it takes about twenty. It's a little chapel for the women of the Abbey you see. Anyway, it was jammed, crammed, blocked. They were standing in the doorway. There were kids there large and small, a splinter of Glastonburians, a few Anglicans, an Anglican parson, and there were our students, all in rows. God! And then there were Liberal Catholics that had come in from so far as Exeter to be there. Oh, it was a great business. More people than they usually get at the regular services. Oh, Lord yes, I should say so.

Anyway, it was hot, it was Midsummer Day, and it was beautiful outside and they felt a little bit chilly so they switched the heater on. The trouble is they forgot to switch it off. Nobody noticed it. And there we were, all fifty of us inside there with a full-blown heater and the sun increasing every minute. By the time we got to the end of that service it was like an oven in there. But even so it was a very good service. I've got a cassette. I'll let you hear a bit of it. You can see what you think of it. But that was that. That was where that was taken. We went back for lunch to my friend's place right at the top of Glastonbury, and we had a buffet lunch out in the garden. That's where I was seated in peace and quiet and that's when someone came along and says, "I want to take a photograph!" So he took it! Hmm. The man you see on the left there, that gaunt looking man, is John Shelly. He was a potter. He used to teach pottery to the troups—you know, to all the artistic people who wanted to learn a bit of pottery and John taught them. And taught a lot of hippies too. He actually owned Chalice Orchard where Dion Fortune lived. He bought it off the people who were there before. Now he's sold it and another lady's bought it, a Mrs. King, I think her name is. And she has it now. But he was the owner before that.

Chapman: Can you tell me something more about when you first met Dion Fortune, when she was just starting the Inner Light?

Butler: She was just starting, just beginning to get the thing going. In 1925 she got the contact from the inner side of things, which made her independent. She had been running a group in conjunction with the Theosophical Society.

Chapman: Do you mean the Christian Mystic Lodge?

Butler: Christian Mystic Lodge, yes, of the T. S. And there was a considerable amount of controversy because the T. S. didn't like the emphasis she placed on the Christian side, you see. And she didn't like the emphasis they'd placed on the Eastern side.

Chapman: She was in the Theosophical Society?

Butler: She was in the T. S. Oh, yes.

Chapman: And in the Golden Dawn? She was in both of these?

Butler: Yes, oh yes. A lot of them were, you know. Brodie-Innes and all those, they were in the T. S., too.

Chapman: I thought that she started the Inner Light to be part of the Golden Dawn, to be an entrance into the Golden Dawn.

Butler: Yes, it was more or less, yes. And then in 1925, she was told from the inner side to go on independently. And she did. It was then that she started out independently, without any reference to the Golden Dawn or to Stella Matutina. But she kept amicable relations with them, and for quite some time there used to be a kind of occasional visitation by Golden Dawn people who used to sit behind a veil in the lodge and watch the ceremonies and sometimes even take part in them. So she never broke with the

Golden Dawn people until Regardie issued his new Golden Dawn stuff, and, of course, then the Golden Dawn immediately practically packed up. Anyway, Mrs. Tranchell-Hayes did. She buried all her stuff in the garden and that was that. It was finished with.

But it wasn't finished with because the cliff got worn down by the sea and fell down. And all her stuff was left on the beach. I remember. I was here then. I remember that I said to— My wife was reading it to Mrs. Poole, who owns the place. She says, "Ah, magical stuff. No, witchcraft stuff, so the paper says. Witchcraft stuff." I said, "Oh, is there a photograph of it?" She says, "Yes." So I took a look. I said, "Good heavens! That has nothing to do with witchcraft. That's a Golden Dawn insignia. That's a sash of a grade and I knew the thing by heart. That has nothing to do with witchcraft. That has something to do with the Golden Dawn, though." And so it was of course. It was Mrs. Tranchell-Hayes's stuff. Hmm.

Well, anyway they sort of passed out, and after that we never heard much from them. We did have a gentleman—what was his name?—Arthur somebody or other. He was what was called a Hibernia Adept. He hopped in once or twice. He was working his own contact and he didn't want to mix up with anybody else's. He was a true Irishman. And he left. But he never joined. But we ceased to hear from him after that. After that the Fraternity of the Inner Light went ahead in its own way. She kept the Chalice Orchard going. But the trouble is, Glastonbury—you'll find when you get down to it—except by car, it's inaccessible. Even in the days of the railway—that railway used to come down but it was so infrequent—you'd get to Bristol and then from Bristol you had to get down. The only other way was to come down by the Great Western Line and get off at Castle Kerry. Then you had to get a taxi to take you about thirteen miles, which was expensive. It could be. So that, one way and the other, they didn't get so many people down. And it took a bit to run the place as a center. So very gradually it tailed off and became just a place where Dion Fortune, Dr. Evans, and the headquarter's people went down on a holiday, you see. And then of course, after her death, the present people began to pull out.

They had got a place at St. Albans but that went down and then they said, "Well, we'll sell this place. " And they sold it. But they sold it to a lady who was already one of the members of the

Inner Light. And she and a dentist who was also a member of the fraternity, they took the place over and ran it on their own. They didn't get anybody in from the outside but they simply used it as where they lived, you see. And they kept going until he passed over, and then she got to a point where she couldn't move about very much. She was too stout and she had heart trouble, too, I think. And she decided to let it go. So she sold it to old John Shelley, and shortly afterward she died. John Shelley took it over and, of course, his wife found Glastonbury far too damp for her liking and John sold it again. So that's how it stands.

That with which Dion Fortune had a great deal to do was, simply well, Chalice Orchard. That was where she let herself go. But that was a purely natural environment. That was a nature contact, Green Ray contact. And they worked the Green Ray contact there. At the bottom of Chalice Orchard they had what was called a sanctuary. It was a big hut, wooden hut. And it had an altar and all the fixings for a little Christian center, you see. And also it could be turned into a Lodge room very easily. The altar moved away and everything else fell into place as a Lodge room. It was a big hut, and it was very well put up and very nicely arranged inside. And there we had lodge meetings and meetings of what was then the religious angle of the Guild of the Master Jesus. And that was there until Robbie and the other lady bought the place. And then at that time the people from London, the Society of the Inner Light people, came down but by that time Dion Fortune had passed on, you see. And they came down and they took everything away, simply took it away as though it were of no further interest. They took everything away.

I've got the cross which was on that altar. It's a Celtic Cross, carved wood. It was carved by one of the close people to Dion Fortune, one of her inner people, and it used to be down at Glastonbury there. I got the chance of getting it when Mr. Chichester was feeling good, and I've got it now, and I'm keeping it. I'm hanging onto it. [Here Mr. Butler brought out the cross. He gave it to me to hold, and I held onto it for several minutes. Later, when I got back to my hotel room, I made a sketch of it from memory.][2] But that was that.

---

[2] This sketch has since been lost.

Then there was a small chalet for Dr. Evans and his wife, Dion Fortune as Mrs. Evans, separate from the main place altogether. And there was another one for Loveday. And then in the main building there were a couple of rooms which used to be booked by somebody else and Miss Lapbury. Then there was an extra piece put on which [served as] a housekeeper's room, or what you like, and that was a kind of self-contained flatlet, put on the side, again in wood. You'll see it if you go into Chalice Orchard. You go up the path and then you turn left. There is a little gate and on your right-hand side is this. It's now in use as a flatlet as a matter of fact, quite a good one. But that was where the housekeeper used to live.

As a matter of fact, that housekeeper came to Southampton to live later. It's curious how these things work around in circles. She and her brother came down to Southampton with his daughter to live and work. I got in touch with her and found out she had been the housekeeper at Chalice Orchard and became friends with her and her brother. Then I suddenly discovered that their father was one of the biggest influences in my adolescent life other than Robert King. He was connected with the healing people, magnetic healers, and he had given me a very great deal of help at a time when I needed it. And there it was, quite curiously enough, we linked up again. His son was a very great help to me when I was starting the church in Southampton until he died.

He and I had an accident in a car. I don't know what the devil happened. We were cruising along nicely outside Salisbury, coming back from Glastonbury, and I woke up, and I looked at the top of something, and I realized that I was looking up at the top of an ambulance. I was inside looking up at the top. I says, "What the devil happened?" All over me broken glass, about ten thousand bits of it. Every time I moved, glass rustled off me. The next thing I knew I was in hospital.

Chapman: What did happen?

Butler: Well, I don't know what happened to this day. But I imagine that Longsdale—that was the chap's name—drew out to overtake at the wrong time, and he smashed dead into something coming along. We were hit in our midship, and our car was crumpled up like a bee, just like that. It was a total write-off. He died later on, but I survived. I haven't got the faintest recollection of what happened. It's a blank. All I know is I woke up in the hospital with a policeman sitting beside my bed. He said, "Can't you remember what happened?" I said, "No. I can't remember a single thing." "Well," he says, "here's a sketch of the thing." And he showed me a sketch of how the cars were lying, and I said, "Nothing in my young life. I know nothing at all about it. All I know is this. I looked at our speedometer and I saw it rated 35 miles an hour, and I must have snoozed off then. But it can't have been much further than that when the crash happened. But all I know is this, I woke up and saw the top of an ambulance and that's all I did. I blacked out again and woke up in the hospital." And that's all that did happen. Of course it shook me up badly and, as I say, it killed him. Not immediately, but it started him away. That was in November, and in December he asked me if I'd go over and celebrate the communion for him. And I did so. I got out—I was convalescing myself—I was crawling in and out of bed; I wasn't properly right. But anyhow, I went over there and I celebrated for him. He used to serve for me, so even sick as he was in his bed we had the celebration in his bedroom. And he tried to serve, to help in the usual way. And then two days later he went. And that was that. I was very lucky. I believe I was lucky because I had a safe seat belt on and also I had a felt hat which came over my eyes, so I didn't get any glass in my eyes. I got it in my cheeks. I was like a pocket with bits of glass and they took them out one by one with a pair of forceps. It didn't leave any lasting trace at all. I was very lucky.

Chapman: I'm curious about something. I've read that Dion Fortune prescribed different courses of training for different people, that she would judge where they were spiritually and then tailor their instruction to their individual needs. Would you go along with this? Did she do this for you?

Butler: Well, she never interfered in my personal life at all. She taught certain principles and then said go to it. If you made a mistake, she gave you a polite ticking off. She never attempted to dominate you. That was my experience. Now I note that Kenneth Grant says that she dominated the lives of her [students]. Well, when I knew her—of course she may have changed, I don't know—but when I knew her she certainly did not. She never attempted to dominate anybody. She simply said, "You work as you're doing and the principles you're breaking will pull you down. But don't worry about me. You'll learn." She would say, "Experience is a very good teacher even though her lessons are rather expensive." Hmm! That was the principle she worked on. Later on she may have changed. I don't know. I can't remember a case either, and we had one or two queer people who came in and went out. No, I can't remember a case where she deliberately interfered with somebody else's life. I think he's entirely off the mark there. Unless she was like that toward the end of her life. I don't know.[3]

You see, in the life of a person, they do change, do alter. Different aspects come out and others go down so that it's always difficult to tell. But all I'd say was that during the time I knew her personally and closely—and that would be a good six years or so, not more—I never knew her attempt to, or teach in the attempt to, dominate in that way. Always she'd say, "Well, if you work along certain principles, you will get your results. If your principles are not right, you'll get the result all right but it won't be the result you want particularly. It's no use me telling you. You've got to find out for yourself." So there it was. You could do it or not do it. That's what annoys me when they say this can't be done and that can't be done. She always was of the opinion that things could be done.

Chapman: Miss Fox gave me the impression that even though people came and went out from Dion Fortune's group, that there were certain permanent members who formed a very close-knit group.

Butler: Very close-knit, yes. Very closely knit. Yes, and we worked hard. And what was more, we obeyed orders. We did what we were told to do.

Chapman: Who made the decisions?

---

[3] The truth is that Kenneth Grant was merely repeating what he had heard from Geoffrey Watkins, son of John M. Watkins, both late of Cecil Court (Watkins Bookshop), London.

Butler: Dion Fortune did. She had the authority. But you see the point is this: Dion Fortune was working with authority and with power. We knew she was a leader, and we knew she had the power. It wasn't a question of second-hand evidence. It wasn't a question of jam yesterday, jam tomorrow, but never jam today. She could produce the goods.

Chapman: And because of this she had the authority?

Butler: Yes. She had two authorities. She had the authority of the Lodge and she had the authority of the fact that, constitutionally built as she was, she was like Mme. Blavatsky. She could produce phenomena at her own will. And that's what a lot of people don't know. But just as Mme Blavatsky could produce an astral [inaudible] and things like that, so could Dion Fortune.

Chapman: Can you give me an example of something like that?

Butler: Yes, I can give you it, but I'm afraid it will have to be off-record.

At this point, I turned the tape recorder off for a while as Mr. Butler spoke of some very personal experiences. When he had finished talking about these experiences, the conversation became general again and he allowed me to turn the tape recorder back on. Here, the tape starts at the point where I had asked him to tell me more about Dr. Theodore Moriarty, the spiritual teacher who had served as the model for Dion Fortune's fictional character "Dr. Taverner."

Butler: Dr. Moriarty was an officer in the England Medical Service in India. Then he came back to England and settled down, and he had a group of people working with him, and he had a place not so far from Guilford. Dion Fortune located it. Within limits, it's somewhere round about there, down about Thursley, just outside Guilford, in *The Secrets of Dr. Taverner*. And he taught these people. If you go back to about that time . . . let's see, when would it be? The thirties roughly. No, the twenties to thirty-three. The occult magazine may carry adverts to his group. But he was very well known through the occult world as a teacher. As a matter of fact, I have quite a lot of his teachings here. I've got a book full of them.

I think it was immediately after the war when Dion Fortune joined him. Now I'm not certain of the date, but I think it was just after the war. She joined him there at this place, and he definitely took her in training. It's from him that she went over to the Golden Dawn people.

Chapman: Was she training with him at the same time that she was taking courses at London University or was that before that?

Butler: No, she was training with him before she started her own things at all. But when she broke with him—and she did break with him—she then continued on her own more or less. She was at that time a member of the T. S. She'd been a member of the T. S. from about the middle of the First World War, the Christian Mystic Lodge of the T. S. And then, of course, she was linked at that time with the East London Clinic for psychoanalytical work. But she thought she might as well put her own particular line forward. Which she did. And it was then that the fun started.

Chapman: This Christian Mystic Lodge existed before she joined it?

Butler: Oh, yes, it existed before she was there.

Chapman: And she turned it into the Inner Light?

Butler: She turned it into her teaching group. And the other Theosophical people didn't like it at all. There was too much which she didn't approve of. It was Western stuff and they were all for Eastern stuff. And the rift began to gather, and finally they tried to throw her out.

At one of the committee meetings, when things were pretty acrimonious, somebody said, "Well, now then, you and the people who think as you do, why don't you get out of the T. S.? Because evidently you are not interested in the T. S. Get out of it." Which is fair enough. When she got home that night, the voice told her. It said, "Well, now what are you waiting for? You've been asked to go, and we told you when you're asked to go, go." So she did. And somewhere or other I've got the document up there that records that. Yes, she said, "I'll go and the karma of the T. S. will be no longer mine." So that was that.

Chapman: Did she take with her the people that were still interested?

Butler: All her students who were in the Christian Mystic Lodge left. Straightaway. And I lectured for the Christian Mystic Lodge some time after they'd gone, and they'd gone back to its old standard of half a dozen people sitting around a gas fire. Whereas, if they'd had the *Inner Light* magazine running they'd have had all kinds of things, because she was quite a go-getter. She was a Yorkshire woman originally, and she knew her business onions, and she really did make a success of it. You take the *Inner Light*, for instance. Have you seen any copies of the *Inner Light*?

Chapman: No.

Butler: Well, I'll show you some presently. The stencil used to be cut by some of the volunteers. Now she had a very great contempt for volunteer effort. She used to say, "If they're a volunteer you can never trust them." She said, "They come in, oh, yes, they're going to do everything, oh, wonderful. But put them down to a humdrum task and they lose interest. And then it's got to be done again by someone else." So as far as she could help it, she wouldn't have volunteer work. But she had to have a bit of it. And I've seen stencils come in which had been cut for the *Inner Light* magazine and she'd look at them, check them through. "No good. Do this again."

"Why, what's wrong with it?"

"Well, this is wrong here, and there are erasures here which haven't been properly erased."

And so forth.

"Oh, but it doesn't look too bad. I thought it would be good enough." She used to open the air on that.

"Only the best is good enough for the Masters." That was her motto all the way through. Only the best is good enough for the Masters. "Take it away and do it again." And very often the whole production of the magazine was held up while that piece was done again. But she wouldn't have it. It wasn't good enough. Her standard was very, very high in regard to that. And so it was with other things.

I used to lecture sometimes. Dion Fortune lectured, A. B. O. lectured, Colonel Seymour, and one or two others. And we used to go down to the library, get an armful of books dealing with the subject we were talking about, and cart them up again. We used to lecture and answer questions and then, "... talking about this lecture, here's a book on the subject, *Astral Projection* by Muldoon and Carrington in the library here. Anybody like to borrow that one?" And somebody would put their hand up. "All right, just see the librarian afterwards." And so we used to get the books in circulation, keep them going.

Well, that would be, say, on Saturday and there would be the meeting of the Guild of the Master Jesus on the Sunday. Well, now then, after the meeting all the chairs were turned around. Everything was cleaned, the place was cleared out, and the little side room was opened up which formed the Sanctuary of the Guild of the Master Jesus. And the altar was set up and everything. Everything was arranged ready for that. And the people who used to do it were all of us who were connected with the group. And then we went home. And then Sunday afternoon when the service had ended, we used to get down to it again, everything cleared from the main lecture room. And we used to roll out a damn huge square of lino which was mapped out in silver and black squares, the lodge floor you see. Out, it used to come over the whole floor. That was that. And then out came the pillows and the altar and everything—the square altar, the cubical altar of the universe. Everything was put up right ready for the lodge meeting on the Monday, just like that.

We had to do that and we did it. We used to come in and do it and go away again. And anybody who felt tired, well, she simply used to say, "Well, all right, forget the way here will you?" They either did it or they didn't do it. If you offered yourself to work for the cause, well you worked for the cause. And if you couldn't get up a little bit earlier or if you didn't like getting your hands dirtied, well it was just too bad. The cause didn't want you. Of course, a lot of people got very annoyed about that. They thought they ought to be able to drift in at odd times and do what they felt they wanted to do and then drift away again. No, it had to be done properly. Everything had to be done in order. She was great on that in those days. Oh yes. Nothing escaped her eagle eye either. It had to be done properly. Anything on the askew had to be put straight. Yes, she was a real disciplinarian in that way. But she never interfered into private lives. I don't understand old Kenneth on that one. Unless she changed very remarkably. Which she may have done.

I was in contact with her until the beginning of the Second World War. In 1942, I was running a Lodge in Guilford under her auspices. She'd given me the permission to run the Lodge and abetted the rituals and everything. And then I had to move from Guilford. I moved down to Petersfield, not too far from here. At the same time the Lodge work up in London went to a standstill practically, owing to the war. The magazine stopped being published. That was the end one, Volume 13. And I believe she began to work on other lines. But of that I know nothing except what Bromage says in that bit of his. But Bromage was inclined sometimes to twist matters to suit his own views.

Chapman: Did you ever live at 3 Queensborough Terrace?

Butler: No, I never lived there. But I was living in London. I had a house just outside London. So I used to drop in now and then.

Chapman: And she had a regular sequence of events, everything was scheduled?

Butler: Oh yes, it was properly systematized. There were lectures throughout the year. And there were lodge meetings—first, second, and third degree Lodges, and all the rest of it. And the Guild of the Master Jesus on Sundays. There was a full program.

Chapman: And the correspondence course, did she keep giving those?

Butler: Oh yes, she did it too, of course.

Chapman: Did you ever meet Dr. Moriarty?

Butler: No, I never met him personally, no. Well, put it this way, I never met him physically, in the physical body. I remember in

1933, possibly, yes, round about there that A. B. O. reported in Lodge that he'd been down and had taken all the bits and pieces of Moriarty's private Lodge and removed them because Moriarty died suddenly of heart trouble. And Dion Fortune had some authority to look after some of his possessions, and A. B. O. went down and saw to it. Got rid of all the magical stuff that was down in Moriarty's place.

Chapman: Did Moriarty ever write any of his teachings down?

Butler: He wrote one book. I'll show you a bit of it.

• • •

The taped ended. It was at this point that Mr. Butler gave me a complete copy of *The Seven Aphorisms of Creation*. As he had explained to me, these were compilations of notes taken at a series of lectures given by Dr. Moriarty. They deal with abstract principles and the idea of a transcendant, abstract Creative Power. They are the real "secrets of Dr. Taverner," the fictitious character Dion Fortune had modeled from Dr. Moriarty for her book of occult mystery stories, *The Secrets of Dr. Taverner*. The content of the lectures were what Dion used as source material when she wrote her book, *Cosmic Doctrine*.

Actually, there are eight aphorisms. They compare pretty closely with the Sephiroth on the qabalistic Tree of Life, of which all are included except, of course, Malkuth.

In her introduction to *Cosmic Doctrine*, Dion Fortune acknowledges her debt to Dr. Moriarty without giving his name:

> This volume of teaching was received from the Inner Planes during 1923 and 1924. The one who gave it is a human being evolved to a very high level. The Personality of his last incarnation is known but it is not revealed, but it may be said that it was of a world-famous philosopher and teacher. In the terminology which is used in esotericism this individual is one of the "Greater Masters."

The foreword to the *Aphorisms* reads partially as follows:

These lectures were given to a small group of students about thirty years ago. Only the Aphorisms themselves were taken down verbatim, these lectures on them, and on the Cosmic Principles, being compilations of notes taken at the time each lecture was given. Unfortunately they were not able to be revised by the Lecturer, but the compilers believe that as here set down, they are true both in letter and in spirit.

The origin of the Aphorisms was not given, but they bear a strong resemblance to the Stanzas of Dzyan and it is not unlikely they are another interpretation of the symbols which were the original fountainhead of the Stanzas.

The interview over, Mrs. Butler served us tea at a little table facing the front window. She then withdrew from the room. I remember the clink of the English china, the heavy tablecloth and napkins, the strong invigorating tea, the soft biscuits and creamy butter and sweet English jelly, and the darling old man at my elbow. And again I remember the feeling of going back in time.

After we ate, Mr. Butler telephoned for a cab. It was getting late and he was obviously very tired. I took a photograph of him in front of the cottage (see figure 3, p. 128), several of the cottage itself and of the immense oak tree, the likes of which I had never seen. We said goodbye as the cab drove up, and I had tears in my eyes because I knew that I would never see Mr. Butler again in this world. Then he looked at me as if he was thinking the very same thought, and I looked at him. And that was that.

The taxi took me back to the guest house, and I thought that the chief part of my adventure was over, but in truth it had only begun.

Southampton, as I have said, is a seaside town. Its history is intimately connected with the sea. In addition, the water in the port has a distinctive pattern of behavior, which some have called a double high tide. Considering Dion Fortune's interest in the magnetic ebb and flow of the tides, this unusual phenomenon is worth describing here:

> One of the greatest assets of Southampton is the pro-
> longed high water maintained for two to three hours
> twice daily.... There is a second flow up the inlet while

Figure 3. *W. Ernest Butler*, on the day of our meeting, January 9, 1974.

there is still slack water from the first flow, and this is followed by one main ebb, the complete occurrence being repeated twelve hours later. The phenomenon is particularly strong at the times of spring and neap tides.

The . . . modern theory of oscillations of the ocean surface appears to lead to the view that this occurrence in Southampton water may be the result of a combination of the coastal character and complicated tidal pulses due to the distortion of the tide as a result of the shallow waters.[4]

Dickmouth, the isolated seaside retreat where Wilfred Maxwell and Miss Le Fay Morgan engaged in their magical workings in Dion's novel, *The Sea Priestess,* is not the name of an actual English town. Richardson says it was meant to be Axbridge and Brean Down in North Wales. However, it bears quite a resemblance to the area around Southampton, particularly to the seaside resort town of Bournemouth.

In any case, to Dion the effect of the moon on the tides was more than a physical phenomenon. It was also a magical one. To her, the moon itself was more than a satellite of the Earth. The moon was a goddess who closely regulated the lives of human beings.

She ruled a kingdom that was neither material nor spiritual. . . . In it moved tides—ebbing, flowing, slack water, high water . . . up and down, backwards and forwards, rising and receding, . . . and these tides affected our lives. They affected birth and death and all the processes of the body.[5]

I would like to say something about the atmosphere of the guest house. It may sound like a far-fetched idea to the reader, but the house's atmosphere was to be intimately associated with Dion Fortune. In fact, I remain convinced that Mr. Butler put me there deliberately.

---

[4] Walter John King, *The British Isles* (London: MacDonald & Evans, 1976) p. 455.

[5] Dion Fortune, *The Sea Priestess* (York Beach, ME: Samuel Weiser, 1972), p. 15.

It was a brick row house on a street not far from downtown Southampton. The proprietress of the establishment was an attractive woman of about 35 years of age. I remember that she was pleasant and friendly and that she wore a floor-length skirt. My room was large, on the second floor at the front of the house. The overall feeling in the room was dampness. Being used to the dry cold of Boston, I felt clammy and damp much of the time.

I hadn't been in my room long. I was going through my papers, looking over *The Seven Aphorisms of Creation*, when I noticed something peculiar about the spreads on the two double beds in the room. The raised chenille was subtly designed in a pattern of waves. The design was so effective that when I looked at it, the pattern seemed to move, replicating the motion of the sea. I actually began to feel queasy looking at it.

I decided to take a bath. Well, the experience of taking a bath in that guest house bathroom was unlike any other I've ever had. Outwardly, it was an ordinary bathroom. But beneath the surface of things, strong primal forces were working. The colors and textures used in the room were iridescent like sandstone and quartz, and every object in the room was a subtle reference to the sea, small references that taken together seemed real—a collection of shells, a jar of beach pebbles, a real sponge, a starfish, and a statue of a mermaid on a shelf. When I got into the old-fashioned bathtub with clawed feet, I felt as if I were being lowered into the bowels of the sea. As the water filled, I felt as if an inner part of my being was sucked into a submarine passageway leading to Neptune's palace and beyond, past every known sonic barrier into the bubbling depths of the universe itself.

There was a sign reminding the visitor to wipe the tub clean after use, and a small can of bathroom cleanser was set on one corner of the tub. I cleaned the tub, feeling as if I were closing down a magical ceremony. Then I went back into my room, put on my nightgown, tights, knee socks, and a sweater and got under the bedcovers.

The night was cold and the morning exceedingly damp. The underwear I had washed out the night before was still wet so, as you can imagine, getting dressed was an unpleasant experience. On top of that, there was the stress of knowing that today (Thursday, January 10) was going to be another big day. Today was the day I would go to Glastonbury.

In the downstairs kitchen, the proprietress cooked and served eggs, ham, and toast for myself and another guest. She showed a polite interest in my plans for the day. I restrained my curiosity about whether she was a practitioner of Wicca or of High Magic because, of course, it was none of my business. After my experience the previous evening in the bathroom, I realized that I was in the house or temple of a sea priestess, perhaps another incarnation of Morgan Le Fay, and I knew Mr. Butler, crafty old magus that he was, had prepared this experience for me.

Chapter 7

Ritual at the Tor: A Glastonbury Pilgrimage

I had already reserved a rental car from a place in downtown Southampton, so I called a cab and away I went. The car rental company turned out to be on the Southampton docks. Everything went smoothly at first. I presented my International Driver's License, and they handed me the keys to the car. But I was a bit taken aback. I had thought, in view of the fact that I was an American, they would show me how to use the car, but they did not and I was too inhibited to ask. I got in and made an effort to calm myself down while I acquainted myself with the controls.

Of course, the steering wheel and all the driver's controls were on the right-hand side of the car. This made me feel disoriented and a little panicky. Nevertheless, I told myself that with practice all would go well. I checked over everything so I knew which buttons did what and then I started the car. It was a frightening experience. I was terrified that I was going to have an accident. Fortunately, I was out on the docks, which afforded an open area where I could experiment. But it was confusing trying to steer in a straight line and to get the car to turn in the direction I wanted it to go. Both the left and right sides of my brain were perplexed, as if I were playing some weird practical joke on each one of them.

At last I gained control of the car and felt ready to get along on my journey. However, at this point I realized that I had no idea in which direction to go. Although I knew where Glastonbury was located in reference to Southampton, I needed a detailed road map of the area. I sensed that I had better find one quickly because the morning was slipping away. I had only the day in which to get to Glastonbury and back.

I drove to the downtown shopping section of Southampton and parked at a meter. I bought a map that covered the area of Southwestern England that I needed. Also I had brought along

The Seven Aphorisms of Creation in the hopes that I might find a copying service. The manuscript was much too long and involved for me to read the night before, but if I got it copied I could take the copy home with me. It was getting late, but I realized I wouldn't pass any larger urban center that day. Tomorrow I would be leaving Southampton, and I had promised Mr. Butler that I would return the manuscript before I left. Time was running out. I located a shop that did copying, and inquired whether it was possible to get the manuscript copied in one day. To my relief they said yes. I left the *Aphorisms* in their keeping—praying no harm would come to them—and struck out on the road for Glastonbury.

Or at least tried to. I figured out which highway I was to get onto, but my efforts to find an entrance to this highway ended me up on the docks again, thoroughly confused. There was no one walking about there from whom to ask directions, no stores, restaurants, or gas stations. So I stopped at the only sign of life, a seaside pub. The place was full of men—dockworkers and sailors. All eyes turned in my direction and immediately there was an enormous amount of leering and rude comments. The common Englishman seemed to be even more primitive in his reactions to women than his American counterpart. Nevertheless, I needed directions, and although the man who gave them to me was drunk, they turned out to be accurate. I finally found myself on the right road even though I was on the wrong side of it!

The highway didn't last very long. Before I knew it I was traveling through the English countryside. By this time I had gotten used to the car, although there were a few times when I almost turned a corner in the wrong direction. I went through several villages and was amazed at how ancient everything looked. The buildings of grey stone, the cobblestone streets, and the background of green fields were straight out of a history book. Before I knew it, I was approaching Glastonbury.

Glastonbury! A peaceful "isle" dotted with apple and other fruit trees and protected from the outside world by a ring of marsh and swampland. Quiet and secluded, it was early regarded as a fairyland or holy place, perhaps as far back as prehistoric times. Known variously as the Isle of Glass and the Isle of Avalon, over the years it acquired many layers of images and associations. St. Joseph of Arimathea, goes the story, traveled there in A.D. 63 to spread the word of Christ. St. Patrick, they say, visited Glastonbury in the fifth century. King Arthur was said to have been transported there after his death.

Legend has it that Joseph was inspired by a vision of the archangel Gabriel to build a church on the tranquil island. Constructing a plain wattle structure, he dedicated it to Mary, the mother of Jesus. Over the centuries, this simple structure was replaced with newer, stronger buildings. A tower and chapel dedicated to St. Michael were erected on Glastonbury's craggy hill, the Tor. During the reign of Ine, King of the West Saxons, a large stone church was built, which, by additions, eventually became the famed Glastonbury Abbey.

Starting as a pious group of twelve monks, the abbey grew to become a prosperous monastic community. The generous gifts of nobles enriched its coffers and expanded its landholdings. The relics and remains of many saints hallowed the altar of the church and attracted hosts of pilgrims. Monks busied themselves with prayer, meditation, fasting, and the copying of manuscripts, their routine punctuated occasionally by visiting royalty or ecclesiastical dignitaries.

Sadly, all this was to end after Henry VIII's dissolution of the English monasteries. Richard Whiting, abbot from 1525 to 1539, was accused of treason and was publicly executed—hung from a gallows on the Tor. Now the abbey's ruins hardly give a hint as to the glory of the old church. Only the tower on the Tor stands, boldly pointing toward the Other World.

Dion Fortune knew Glastonbury like the back of her hand. She knew the names of its plants and trees, she knew its roads, marshes, apple orchards, meadows, and moors. She knew its architecture and its history, real and imaginary.

In reading her book, *Glastonbury: Avalon of the Heart*, we reap the fruits of Dion's erudition. The legends of Merlin and the Grail, of the saints of the Celtic Church, of Joseph of Arimathea, and of the Glastonbury of the monks and the abbey all come alive for us. What is more, all the physical aspects of Glastonbury evoked symbolic and mystical associations for Dion. Due to her psychic sensitivity, we can glimpse what she calls, "Avalon of the Heart, a land known only to the eye of vision."

Dion also brings us up to date on happenings in Glastonbury in her own time. She tells of Alice Buckton who purchased the abbey monastery at an auction. Miss Buckton converted the

Figure 4. Glastonbury Tor, January 10, 1974.

monastery into a guest house and there produced her mystery play, *Eagerheart*. This annual performance attracted many people to the town. Dion also tells of the mystical play, *Immortal Hour* by Fiona Macleod, which, with music added by the composer Rutland Boughton, was produced as an opera in the Assembly Rooms of Glastonbury; of the Arthurian dramas of Reginald Buckley; and of the *Little Plays of St. Francis* by Laurence Housman, also produced in the Assembly Rooms.

Finally, she relates the story of Frederick Bligh Bond, the archaelogist and ecclesiastical architect, who discovered the buried chapel of the great Saxon King Edgar beneath the abbey ruins. Bond claimed to have been directed by communications from a dead monk. His two books, *The Gate of Remembrance* and *The Hill of Vision*, describing the excavations, brought more curious pilgrims to Glastonbury. Eventually, the town became a center for artists and craftsmen of all kinds, until in Dion's day it was experiencing a veritable cultural renaissance.

According to Dion, there were three roads to Glastonbury: the high road of history, the upland path of legend, and the secret Green Road of the soul.

I searched for the house belonging to Mr. and Mrs. Snowden, the people to whom Mr. Butler had given me a letter of introduction. They weren't at home. I left a note in the door saying I had been by and would probably come again. Then I proceeded toward the Tor (see figure 4).

I drove to the foot of it, got out of the car, and stood for awhile to get oriented and to absorb the atmosphere. It was cold and windy and the hill had a grey, ethereal quality. So this was the spot said in medieval legend to be the earthly entrance to the underworld. I felt very quiet in my inmost being and at one with everything around me.

As I started up the hill, a man came up to me and asked if I lived in Glastonbury. When I said no, that I was just a tourist, he looked surprised and said that I looked like a native. I'm sure he made that mistake because I was dressed in a long gray tweed skirt, a pale brown sweater under a dark green cardigan, and a pair of brown leather boots.

I proceeded up the hill and stood a long time on the summit, observing the old stone tower and appreciating the view of the surrounding countryside. The only other people present were the man who had stopped me and his two companions. I waited till they had descended again, and then I went up close to the monument and performed the Cabalistic Cross Ritual. The Hebrew Names of Power seemed oddly at home here. And then I thought to myself that this was the realm of Magic where symbols of all belief systems merge. I stood within the Magic Circle drawing power into myself until I felt a concentration of force, a purging of the spirit, and a desire to go on with my quest. I stood there for quite a long time before I descended the hill.

Figure 5. Dion's cottage at Chalice Orchard, Glastonbury.

At the foot of the hill was Chalice Orchard and the house in which Dion Fortune had lived (see figure 5). Mr. Butler had telephoned the people who were the present owners of the house, so they were expecting me when I knocked on the door. Mr. Shelly answered, smiled, and asked me in. Well, there I was standing inside the very house in which Dion Fortune had lived! It was a strange feeling, indeed. I felt as if I was actually *there*, as if Dion herself would be coming in at any moment to welcome me to the fold.

Mr. Shelly introduced me to his woman friend and invited me to sit down. He offered me tea. I sat down on the sofa and looked around the room. Mr. Shelly explained where everything had been located when Dion Fortune lived there. He showed me where the altar had been. In my mind I pictured the cross that Mr. Butler had shown me on top of the altar.

Figure 6. A photograph from the booklet Mr. Shelly gave me of the grounds of Chalice Orchard below the house on the north end.

We talked for quite a while about Dion Fortune, the house, and about Glastonbury, past and present, until finally I realized it was time for me to go. The afternoon was getting on and I was afraid of having to drive back in the dark. Mr. Shelly gave me a little booklet containing photographs of the house, which he explained was soon to be put up for sale (see figure 6). Taken in the early spring of 1973, the pictures showed north and south views of the house with Chalice Hill in the background surrounded by apple trees, walnut trees, a plum tree, a quince and peach trees, and a California yucca tree, as well as a splendid view from the breakfast room window of the Vale of Avalon (see figure 7, p. 140).

I thought of Dion Fortune's followers sitting at the long refectory table with the scent of peat burning at the open hearth. As I imagined the scene I could almost feel the peace and warmth

Figure 7. Another photograph from the booklet. This one is a view out of the Breakfast Room window of the cottage as we look toward the Vale of Avalon.

generated by the close-knit group, by the love and trust they had for each other, and by their sense of dedication to a lofty goal. Dion often said her path was not the Path of the Hearth-Fire, yet here at Glastonbury she had truly created a family and a home. There was good Magic at work here. You could still feel it.

My visit to Chalice Orchard was the climax of my adventure, the true end of my quest. Everything afterward was to be a downward spiral.

It was already beginning to get dark as I left Glastonbury. I drove a little faster than I had earlier, as I felt more confident with the car, but by the time I was halfway back to Southampton it was pitch dark. I remember passing the sign pointing to the turnoff for Stonehenge. It seemed odd to see that name out of Britain's prehistory painted in the fluorescent letters of a highway sign. I thought fleetingly of taking the turnoff but quickly dismissed the idea. It was dark, it was late, and I was very low on gas—petrol, rather. I was already worried about whether I had enough to get back to the guest house and return the car in the morning. So I missed out on Stonehenge. The ancient druidic temple must have been an impressive sight at that hour, in the moonlight, but I had come in quest of Dion Fortune and Glastonbury, not the Druids, and so I headed straight on. Someday, maybe I'd go back and see what I missed.

Chapter 8

FORTUNE AND CROWLEY: KENNETH GRANT REMINISCES

It was too late to return the car that night so I parked it on the street outside the guest house, hoping it wouldn't be stolen during the night. I set my travel alarm for early the next morning. I had to return the car as soon as the car rental place opened and catch the first train to London in order to make my eleven o'clock appointment with Kenneth Grant. I also had to pick up the manuscript of the *Aphorisms* at the copy service and return the original to Mr. Butler.

After returning the car, I took a cab to the copy place, then I went back to the guest house and gave the original manuscript to the proprietress, telling her it was important that she return it to Mr. Butler for me. That done, I told the cab driver to make all haste to the train station.

When I got off the train in London, I took a taxi to the Charles Dickens Hotel where I had reserved a room for my last night in London. No more second-class accommodations; I wanted to spoil myself. I requested that my suitcase be taken up to my room, and I went directly out again and had the bellman hail me a cab.

Mr. Grant lived in a suburban district on the outskirts of the city. I had forgotten that he had told me he was on the tube line. I was running short of time anyway; it was almost 11:00 (Mr. Grant had cleverly manipulated our meeting to occur on the 11th day of January at 11 o'clock. It wasn't until much later that I discovered that the number *eleven* is the sacred number of the Left-Hand Path.)

I was nervous—you could even say scared—about meeting Kenneth Grant. After all, he had been Aleister Crowley's secretary. Furthermore, he was an authority on Tantric Magic. Who knows what type of sinister rites were performed at his house? I imagined being detained against my will and forced to be the priestess in some carnal ritual. By the time the cab drew up in front of his house, my imagination had played out every possible scenario.

My fears were not quelled when, in answer to my ring, Mr. Grant opened the door and in a low, ceremonious tone said, "Do What Thou Wilt!" I was reminded of Dion Fortune's novel, *The Demon Lover*, when the heroine, Veronica Mainwaring, was admitted to the house of Lucas, the vampire, secretary of an occult fraternity. But rather than give the expected response, i.e., "Love is the Law, Love Under Will," I merely smiled and said an ordinary American hello. Instead of throwing me out for blaspheming (a possibility I did entertain), he ushered me into his comfortable abode.

Mr. Grant showed me into a sitting room on the first floor. There he left me alone, saying something about letting me "collect myself." I looked around the room. There were several articles of fine furniture, an oriental rug, walls lined with bookshelves. The atmosphere of the room reminded me of Lucas's waiting room in *The Demon Lover*, a room "full of strange, almost electrical vibrations." Was Grant's resemblance to Lucas only superficial, I wondered? Or was he also a "man of dark and unknown purposes" who would use me "unscrupulously for his own ends?"

Mr. Grant did not want to be taped, so I put the tape recorder, unplugged, under my chair. I took notes during the interview and afterward, as soon as I got back to my hotel.

We had sherry and what the English call biscuits (known to Americans as cookies), served on a table beside a window with a view of a garden at the back of the house. As it turned out, Mr. Grant was an attractive, well-mannered, well-dressed man in his forties, intelligent, cultivated, and friendly. Now and then I was reminded of Lucas' "peculiar sense of poise and power," but he treated me in every way with courtesy and respect, and he never turned into a werewolf or a vampire. He sat opposite me and we talked for several hours of Crowley, Dion Fortune, the Inner Light, and related subjects.

Mr. Grant told me about his first meeting with Dion Fortune, which took place in January or February of 1945. Aleister Crowley was living in the boardinghouse, Netherwood, in Hastings, Sussex, where he spent his last days. As I have already mentioned, Mr. Grant served as his secretary. Crowley sent Grant to the train station to pick up Dion. Mr. Grant said that he remembered her as very old and sick-looking, thin and emaciated. She wore a beige cape and a large, brass sun medallion. She was also wearing a lot of rings and "other things." He said that she stood out from the rest of the crowd at the station. He also said that the taxi driver looked as if he thought he was picking up something from outer space. She appeared to be looking forward eagerly to seeing Crowley, Grant said, although she had met him previously.

> She was close to death and had lost much of [her] physical force and vigour. . . . Even so, she conveyed (transmitted would be a better word) a tremendous psychic vitality which struck me very forcibly at the time.[1]

When Grant and Dion arrived at the rooming house, Crowley was with Frieda Harris, the artist who designed the Crowley Tarot Deck. Dion took off her cape. Underneath she was wearing a tan shirt and a jacket with panels of suede or leather. My notes say that Crowley and Harris were looking over "the Tarot rejects," probably the drawings not selected for inclusion in the pack. Mr. Grant said that they were painting-size, that Crowley, Frieda, and Dion were looking at them, and that Dion admired them. Among other things, Mr. Grant heard them talking about "two black cocks." Further, he says that he well remembers Dion's zest in discussing with Crowley the possibility of reviving the pagan attitudes to cosmic and elemental forces. Louis Umfraville-Wilkinson, a writer and co-literary executor with John Symonds for Aleister Crowley, was also present on that occasion.

At the second meeting between Fortune and Crowley at which Mr. Grant was present, Mr. Grant didn't hear the conversation. He had gone downstairs with Grady McMurtry, later the California representative of the O.T.O., who had come over on his leave to see Crowley and found him with Dion Fortune. Mr. Grant said Dion saw Crowley several times that year, but he was present only on these two occasions. The second meeting had to have occurred before June of 1945, when Grant left Netherwood. In Kenneth Grant's latest book, *Remembering Aleister Crowley*, he points out that he was so preoccupied at the time with copying Crowley's

---

[1] Kenneth Grant in a letter to the author dated August 9, 1973, which is reprinted earlier in this book.

manuscripts that he didn't pay very close attention to the many interesting visitors Crowley received at Netherwood. Grant says he does remember, however, that Dion sent Crowley a copy of her novel, *The Sea Priestess,* in June of 1944.

Considering Mr. Grant's physical description of Dion at that time, it seems likely that during this last year of her life (she died in January of 1946), either the leukemia had already set in or other degenerative symptoms had commenced. Perhaps the blood poisoning from the tooth was only part of an infection that was taking over her entire body. Obviously, since I am not a medical doctor, I can only speculate in a general way about Dion's final illness. In any case, Dion was no longer the robust woman pictured in her marriage photograph and remembered by her friends and associates. Apparently, in 1945 she was losing weight and losing it rapidly.

Mr. Grant feels the reason for the Inner Light's rejection of Dion Fortune was the interest she had developed in the subject of Tantric Magic. He bases his opinion on her writings, on the conversation he overheard that day in the rooming house, and on the content of one of Dion's letters to Crowley. This letter was dated March 14, 1945. It is quoted in *Remembering Aleister Crowley* (page 33) and is reproduced on p. 153.

Bernard Bromage, a scholar and lecturer, who himself translated some of the Hindu Tantric texts and knew Dion Fortune very well over a number of years, affirms Dion's interest in Tantra. In particular, he says, she was interested in the interplay between mind and body. He states that "she saw quite exceptionally clearly, the close connection between modern empiricism and tried and tested tenets of the great Tantric and Kabbalistic ritualists."[2]

Dion Fortune's book, *The Esoteric Philosophy of Love and Marriage,* first published in 1924 when she was 32, goes into detail on her opinions on the esoteric concept of sex and the subject of sexual polarity. In this book, she refers to sex magic as "one of the most potent forms of magic that exists." She goes on to say:

> For the use of the greater potencies and the operations of the higher occultism, it is necessary to have a pair

---

[2] Bernard Bromage,"Dion Fortune." *Light* (Spring, 1960).

> working in polarity; only so can the great cosmic voltages
> be carried without the danger of "earthing."[3]

She also knew the risks involved.

> If a sensual thought intrude into consciousness at a time
> when the channels are open and the forces are flowing,
> those forces will immediately follow the focus of atten-
> tion, and the result will be outbreak of passion and
> sensuality.[4]

There is the evidence in Dion's novels. All of them involve magical work between a couple, and power created through a polarity
that is sexual in origin, regardless of the fact that no overt sex is
described. This quote from *The Sea Priestess* is a good example:

> Then I saw why there must be priestesses as well as
> priests; for there is a dynamism in a woman that fecun-
> dates the emotional nature of man as surely as he fecun-
> dates her physical body.[5]

Sex in her novels is never described graphically; it is always
hinted at shyly. One gets the picture of a keenly curious schoolgirl
or a sheltered married woman with a rich fantasy life. What we see
is an intense and vital interest in one of the more obscure and
exotic branches of the occult by a woman whose own sexual behavior was markedly traditional. That she was a virgin until her late
thirties, as Alan Richardson says, is highly likely. That she was faithful to her husband is clear from the evidence. That sex was infrequent during their married life is probable. Yet she had the courage,
during the last year of her life, to make contact with someone of
Crowley's reputation in order to more fully comprehend this area
of interest. I think this showed courage and dedication to the Work.
In spite of one's feelings regarding sex magic, we owe Dion Fortune
the highest admiration for this quest of her latter days. How unfortunate that we cannot read her personal diary or letters of that period

---

[3] Dion Fortune, *The Esoteric Philosophy of Love and Marriage* (London: Aquarian Press, 1988), pp. 88-89, 91.
[4] Dion Fortune, *The Esoteric Philosophy of Love and Marriage*, p. 93.
[5] Dion Fortune, *The Sea Priestess*, p. 187.

or at least the novel she may have been working on. Its images and message we shall never know.

In *The Story of Dion Fortune,* Fielding and Collins claim that Dion Fortune began experiments using magical polarity sometime before 1939, exactly when is not known. *Sea Priestess,* Dion's novel in which the main character, Vivien Le Fay Morgan, tries a magical polarity experiment with Wilfred Maxwell, the book's "hero," was first published in 1938. The polarity experiments continued to a lesser extent during the Second World War (1939-1945). Practices of this type were restricted to the higher grades under oaths of secrecy. Some of these experiments culminated in physical sex between the priest and priestess. After Dion's death, the polarity experiments continued under the leadership of Arthur Chichester who claimed to be receiving direction from Dion Fortune from the Inner Planes. These workings continued until about 1949 when the society was reorganized along different lines. A thorough discussion of the magical polarity workings can be found in the chapter titled "Sexual Polarity" in Charles Fielding's *The Story of Dion Fortune.*

Grant feels strongly that Dion was interested in this aspect of magic. In his article on Dion Fortune in *Man, Myth & Magic,* he states his belief that in *Moon Magic* and *The Sea Priestess,* Fortune's heroine was a priestess of the Black Isis. He defines the Black Isis as "the primordial and elemental essence of Woman in her power aspect."

> Black Isis embodies the *sakti* (power) that destroys all that is inessential and obstructive to the soul's development. It is the power that liberates the spirit of man from the confines of limited experience. The basis of Fortune's practical work involves the bringing through into manifestation of this sakti, by the magically controlled interplay of sexual polarity. This is embodied in the priest, or consecrated male, and the specially chosen female. Together they enact the immemorial Rite and form a vortex in the ether, down which the tremendous energies of Black Isis rush into manifestation.[6]

---

[6] Kenneth Grant, "Dion Fortune" *Man, Myth and Magic,* Issue #36 Volume 8, (New York: Marshall Cavendish, 1970), p. 1023.

Furthermore, he feels that Dion's most significant contribution lies in her calling attention to the kalas or magical emanations in their relation to the endocrine system, which in turn relates to the subtle anatomy of the chakras and the Kundalini Shakti, as the dormant power in the occult dimensions of consciousness. Grant goes so far as saying, "It was obvious to me then, and the conviction grows stronger each time I read anything by her, that Dion saw herself as *the* magical shakti of the New Aeon."[7]

Whether or not Dion saw herself in this role, the evidence indicates without a doubt that Dion Fortune was interested in Tantric Magic during most of her active magical life. This interest continued during the year that she was failing physically.

Fielding and Collins mention the public lecture at which Dion first encountered Crowley. This is probably the same lecture Helah Fox told me about when I interviewed her at Evelyn Heathfield's studio. These two authors say that the lecture took place at "The Belfry," the house said to have been the prototype of the church in Dion's novel, *Moon Magic*.

> Dion entered the room with some of her friends to find Crowley already seated there in the company of two of his scarlet women. He got up (an uncharacteristic gesture) and bowed to her. She replied with a curt British bow and passed on to her seat.[8]

This description fits in well with that of Helah Fox, her account merely relating additional material on the same incident. Miss Fox's account of the lecture, however, shows Crowley trying to introduce himself to her by giving her one of his books, which she refuses. Also, Miss Fox said that Dion didn't realize that Crowley was there until the middle of her lecture. Both Miss Fox's account and that of Fielding, however, do agree that Dion had known who Crowley was before she saw him at the lecture hall. Whatever the exact sequence of events at that lecture, this meeting stimulated the beginning of a correspondence between the two.

---

[7] Kenneth Grant in a letter to the author dated August 9, 1973.

[8] Charles Fielding and Carr Collins, *The Story of Dion Fortune* (Dallas, TX: Star & Cross, 1985), p. 156.

The meetings at Crowley's rooming house in 1945 and the encounter in the London lecture hall are the only documented meetings I know of between Aleister Crowley and Dion Fortune.

The meetings at the rooming house took place in 1945. It was in 1944 that she sent Crowley a copy of *The Sea Priestess*. The earliest existing letter from her to him is dated January 1942, exactly four years before her death. A reading of it gives the definite impression that they had been corresponding for some time since it resembles a sort of comfortable, friendly chat. Since the first known letter between the two is dated 1942, I would guess that the lecture encounter took place in 1940 or 1941.

Alan Richardson in *Priestess* says that "Present-day Crowleyans . . . affirm quite strongly but with no hard evidence that Dion once worked magic with the Great Beast, The Logos of the Aeon" (p. 152). He is right. She did *not* work magic with him. She met, visited, and corresponded with him over a period of four or five years. She owned (and probably read) most of his books. In the introduction to the first edition of *The Mystical Qabalah* (1935), she admitted being indebted to his work. But if she worked magic with him on the occasions when Mr. Grant was not present, The Logos said nothing of it to his secretary, and no other witnesses have come forth with their testimony.

Richardson says further: "She herself denied ever having met him." This denial undoubtedly was voiced *before* she met him, since she met him so late in her life. It wasn't a "fib" as Richardson suggests.

Finally, there is the matter of the Fortune-Crowley correspondence that Grant mentioned in his first letter to me. Before I left on the day of our meeting, Mr. Grant showed me the only one of these letters he possessed. It is dated March 27, 1945, and is addressed to Dion at 2[1] Queens[borough] Place, London. Mr. Grant allowed me to make a handwritten copy of this letter. Another, earlier letter (dated January 8, 1942), this time from Dion to A.C., is in The Warburg Institute Archives at the University of London. Part of a third letter, also from Dion to A.C. and dated March 14, 1945, was copied by Grant into his diary while he was working for Crowley at Netherwood. The letters are reproduced on pages 151-153.

A.C.—D.F.   27 March 1945
                    Dion Fort., 2 Queens Pl. W.1

Dear D.F.
    93

I am very much concerned indeed at what you tell me. It is your second near escape and I really think it might be a warning. I have never been a partisan of the Hero Martyr School. The Captain should not be the last person to be saved or go down with the ship. He is the person to be saved first because he is the best witness as to the causes of the accident and that may be valuable to the cause of navigation in general.

I am sorry that you should have fallen on to the gainsaying of St. Thomas. On my walk through China I was three or four days inside the Frontier when I was met by poor dear Litton, our Consul at Teng-yuck. We sat down and had lunch together. He had the reputation of running the whole Province of Yunnan by sheer force of personality and I was naturally anxious to [illegible]. I began by remarking that I had been told a lot of absurd stories and attached no credit to them. He pulled me up sharp—"Young man!" he said very solemnly, "the first thing to remember when you're in China is confirmation of Poule-aux-Rats story from 50 people you could meet in pubs and clubs within 1/2 mile radius of your headquarters."

By a strange coincidence I picked up a copy of "Pitcher in Paradise" in a second-hand shop here, and just as on to page 286. It is a story of Sheffield in which a big monkey was backed to break a noted terrier's rat-killing record of one hundred inside 4 minutes. Pitcher gives all possible details except the size of the Pit, but the monkey won by 76 seconds after a very slow start. Your analogy of your adventure with a mouse is not relevant. The behavior of a frightened animal is very different to that of a fighting animal excited by the smell of blood.

If that is not enough evidence for you, I give up. But it certainly happened. I was myself present on three occasions. The first introduced by an expert in strange doings and afterwards as myself in charge of a party.

I do hope you will take my advice and get well outside range until we have driven the Hun out of the Hague and neighborhood despite all that bishop can do.

93/

93

93

3, Queensborough Terrace
W.2.
8th January, 1942.

Dear 666,

Many thanks for your letter and card. I am glad you find my tabernacles pleasant. I saw designs for two of your Tarot trumps at the Atlantis Book Shop when calling upon Michael Juste, and thought them very fine. I should be interested to know when they are published. I have, I think, most of your books, but not 'Thumbs up'.

I am afraid my Biblical knowledge has grown rusty and I cannot follow the reference to Daniel and the Apocalypse with regard to Mr. Churchill, so you will have to dot the I's if you want to convey anything to my intelligence, which you over-estimate. Is Mr. Churchill to be conceived of as crowned with the stars, or does his tail draw the twelfth part of them after him?

My mentality always has hampered my work, and, I am afraid, always will.

With all good wishes for the success of your Tarot, which certainly deserves it.

Yours sincerely,

Dion Fortune

Mr. Grant forgot to show me the third letter when I visited him in 1974. He has since sent it to me. This third partial letter also appears in Grant's new book, *Remembering Aleister Crowley* (Skoob Books, London, 1991) and I quote it here.

She had sent him a copy of her novel *Sea Priestess* in June 1944. On March 14th 1945 she had written to him: "The acknowledgement I made in the introduction to *The Mystical Qabalah* of my indebtedness to your work, which seemed to me no more than common literary honesty, has been used as a rod for my back by people who look on you as Antichrist. I am prepared to dig in my toes and stand up to trouble if I have got to, but I don't take on a fight if I can help it nowadays because it wastes too much time. I am fully aware that there *will* come a time when I shall have to come out into the open and say: this is the law of the New Aeon, but I want to pick my time for that, because I propose to be in a strong strategic position when I do so, and if you give Mrs. Grundy advance information, I may not be properly entrenched when the inevitable blitz starts. Therefore I ask you not to mention my name for the present. I am at work on a book on the paths. . . ."

On March 19th, 1946, Crowley wrote to Louis Wilkinson: . . . "Dion Fortune is dead. There was a very secret understanding, by which she acknowledged my authority. . . ."

It is interesting to note that both Grant and Symonds claim there was a "stack" of letters, whereas Helah Fox told me she doubted there were so many. I tend to believe the accounts of Grant and Symonds. Both say they saw a stack of letters at Symonds' apartment in Hampstead, London where the letters, along with Crowley's other papers and effects, were brought after Crowley's death and where the letters and papers were stored for some time. Grant met Symonds at Crowley's funeral and afterwards collaborated with Symonds in editing and annotating several of Crowley's works, foremost of which are *The Confessions of Aleister Crowley* and *The Magical Record of the Beast 666.*

Recently, when I wrote to Kenneth Grant requesting permission to print the letter in this book, he suggested I write to John Symonds regarding what happened to the other letters. I immediately wrote to Mr. Symonds and shortly after received his reply (dated January 29, 1991). I quote the following portions of Mr. Symonds' letter:

> Within a few days of Aleister Crowley's death in 1947, all his goods and chattels, including his paintings and archive of diaries and letters, were delivered to my flat in Hampstead, London. Among the letters were . . . a fair quantity of letters from Dion Fortune with carbon copies of Crowley's replies to her. I held onto this archive for three years, then I dispatched it to Karl Germer of New York who had been Crowley's main financial support since the mid 20s and who is described in Crowley's will as the Grand Treasurer General of the Order of Oriental Templars. . . . I confess to my shame that I hardly read Dion Fortune's letters to Crowley . . . being unaware of their importance.
>
> Germer died in 1962 and his wife, Sasha, became the custodian of the Crowley archive: the Germers had long

moved out of New York to an area where Charles Manson was living and one night Manson and his "family" broke into Mrs. Germer's house and stole the whole archive of Crowley's letters, as well as books and diaries of Crowley. Among the Manson "family" was a young boy who, through being tiresome, was one night locked up in a chest while the rest of them went out. The child managed to get out of the chest and in a rage set the whole house alight. Thus the whole Dion-Crowley correspondence was destroyed. That is the account I was told.

You will probably think, "Ah, what a mine of valuable information I have lost through not seeing the Crowley-Dion Fortune correspondence!" But I believe that if you could read those letters you would be disappointed. I'm sure you have read *Magick Without Tears*, a collection of Crowley's letters to one Anne Macky in which the Beast explains nothing about magic and is tiresomely verbose and irrelevant. His letters to Dion Fortune must have been in the same vein, being written about the same time; and her letters to him were, I'm sure, guarded and contained little or nothing personal.[9]

In fact, the letter reproduced on page 151, now the only remaining letter from Crowley to Dion Fortune, is much as Symonds speculated and fits perfectly with what is known of Crowley's personality. He talks mostly about himself, using the letter as an excuse to tell an autobiographical anecdote. His remark about the Captain and his ship is a pathetic attempt to defend an act of cowardice and shows Crowley's immunity to positive human values. Naturally Crowley could never identify with a hero, i.e., someone who shows great courage for an altruistic cause, someone supremely noble or self-sacrificing. His patronizing remark to Dion toward the end of the letter is also typical: "Your analogy of your adventure

---

[9] In a postcard the author received from Mr. Symonds dated January 31, 1991, he called her attention to page 568 of his book, *The King of the Shadow Realm*, which quotes an extract from Crowley's diary for 1944: "18 May. Wrote Dion Fortune with P [rospectus of *The Book of Thoth*]."

with a mouse is not relevant." It is the tone of a man who *needs* to appear the superior in his relationships with women.

In contrast Dion certainly did not *need* Crowley, and right from the first she appears to be her usual strong and independent self in her dealings with him. Even though in the meetings at Crowley's boardinghouse Dion was in all probability dying, she does not show herself to be the pathetic "jilted woman" drawn by Richardson. In spite of her declining health she was pursuing her magical interests, delving into an area of the occult certainly not the province of shy virgins or chaste spinsters. Yet she did not get sucked into Crowley's circle. She came, observed, conversed, and left—richer for the contact and wiser for the information.

Dion's two letters to Crowley, however, are not quite so guarded as John Symonds supposed. In the fragment dated 1942 she says that he overestimates her intelligence! She also makes this self-derogatory statement: "My mentality always has hampered my work, and, I am afraid, always will." Quite honestly, I feel that Dion made this statement for the same reason she acknowledged her indebtedness to his work. Crowley was sixteen years her senior, which tended to create a sort of father-daughter or male-teacher-female-pupil relationship. The self-derogatory statement can be ascribed to this relationship dynamic, but also, I hate to admit, to the nauseating way many intelligent women used to deprecate themselves and minimize their accomplishments and abilities when in the presence of the "all-powerful male." Some progress has been made in this area since then. More women are asserting themselves and fewer are playing Cinderella. But in spite of the women's movement, this problem still exists. That Dion Fortune did this does not reflect negatively on her strength of character or self-esteem; it only shows that she was not immune to negative cultural conditioning.

After Dion's death, Crowley commented to Louis Wilkinson in a letter dated March 19, 1946 (also published in *Remembering Aleister Crowley*): "There was a very secret understanding, by which she acknowledged my authority. . . ." Personally, I don't believe a word of it.

Richardson's description of Dion Fortune after her split with Penry Evans as a "woman alone" and "the Moon Priestess who had no light of her own" is somewhat distasteful. But I found his statement on page 201 particularly offensive: "Poor, poor Dion . . . what is she trying to tell us here, at the age of forty-five, when the menopause had begun, and her husband was more and more likely to leave as the days went by?" How could Richardson know whether or not menstruation had in fact ceased in Dion's body at age 45 and, if so, whether it had any effect on her? Menopause can occur as early as 45, but it usually occurs at about age 50 or sometimes as late as 55.

In any case, contrary to popular belief, menopause is natural and takes place smoothly for most women. Many women welcome menopause because it means not having any more menstrual periods or concern about pregnancy. Eighty percent of women experience no other signs of menopause besides the cessation of menstruation. Only twenty percent report symptoms severe enough to seek medical attention. The fatigue, heart palpitations, and depression reported by some women during this time may be symptoms of menopause in some cases but there is wide disagreement about this. There is no specific mental disorder associated with menopause, and research shows that women experience no more depression during these years than at other times. Tension or depression can occur at any stage, but when these states occur during menopause there is a tendency to blame the menopause process. Perhaps it was simply Richardson's male perspective that colored his usual keen perspective of Dion's inner life.

Helah Fox, the Inner Light member who was with Dion at 3 Queensborough Terrace the day Penry Evans left, quoted Dion's exact words to her on that occasion: "Well, the time has come and Merl has left. And that's the end. I feel it will be a shock to some people to know that this has happened but it's just like a leaf withering and falling off." No tears, no sentimentality, just a simple statement of the facts. "It's just like a leaf withering and falling off." This is not the cry of a woman with a broken heart, in anguish over the loss of her man. It is the comment of one who has known all along that the separation was coming, and who had accepted, perhaps even welcomed it.

Fielding and Collins, whose information about Penry and Dion's married life seems to come from fairly intimate sources, conclude that, "As far as is known, the separation between the two of them was amicable."[10]

> At no time, was there any danger of her losing control of the organization. . . . Despite what various commentators have said about Dion Fortune being a spent force, the fact is that late in the 30s, at the beginning of the war, it was Dion Fortune who remained firmly in control and Colonel Seymour and Christine Campbell Thomson and Penry Evans who went.[11]

It was natural that she turned inward after Penry was gone. Many people do after a marital separation, in order to reevaluate their priorities and experience themselves as individuals once again. But if the marriage has been rocky—as Dion's was—there is usually an accompanying feeling of relief and a new sense of freedom.

I don't think it's wise to read too much autobiography into the characters and events in her novels. It is better to stick to the facts of her life as we know them. All the evidence indicates that Dion's mind was as keen at this time as ever, filled with that fervent intellectual curiosity that had spurred her on throughout her life. She became involved in the new Spiritualist movement both as a medium and as a lecturer. She reopened the Outer Court of the Inner Light to draw in new members. She established new contacts with authorities in the occult world and attempted to organize a collaborative venture. She was also working on a nonfiction book, *The Psychological Qabalah*.[12] Some believe she was also working on another novel to be called *Sun Magic*.[13] These activities, along with her explorations into Tantra suggest the same active personality, albeit in a body weakened by illness. It is possible her followers had ceased to stimulate her. And perhaps she didn't so much lose her contacts as cease to need them anymore.

Richardson minimizes Dion's study of psychology, yet it was one of the enduring passions of her life. His remark about her book,

---

[10] Charles Fielding and Carr Collins, *The Story of Dion Fortune*, p. 93.

[11] Charles Fielding and Carr Collins, *The Story of Dion Fortune*, p. 148-149.

[12] Dion Fortune, *Psychic Self-Defense*, Publisher's Note.

[13] The author was told this by Kenneth Grant. The Inner Light has declined to answer any questions on the subject.

The Machinery of the Mind, is both irreverent and disturbing. He says, "It makes dismal reading today, but that is hardly her fault. It is not so much that her psychology was trivial or shallow: the problem is that psychology itself is trivial and shallow." With one gesture, Richardson tosses away the lifework of countless selfless and dedicated medical researchers and practitioners.

Certainly Freud, Jung, and Adler theorized too much. Freud, starting as a student of neurology, grew frustrated with the lack of information available in that field to answer the questions that plagued him about the human mind. So he dreamed up the way he thought things might or ought to be.

But neurology has progressed a long way since then. Basic knowledge about brain chemistry has increased substantially since the 1940s. The conditions of depression and mania have been found to be physiologically based and genetically linked. Chemical compounds known as neurotransmitters—substances that allow communication between nerve cells—are thought to be involved in the development of schizophrenia. It is likely that the disorder is associated with some imbalance in the complex, interrelated chemical systems of the brain.

Furthermore, discoveries in the field of psychopharmacology have created a revolution in psychiatric circles. Psychotropic medications have been developed that improve the balance of chemical substances within the brain and relieve the symptoms of mental illnesses more quickly and effectively than ordinary psychotherapy or psychoanalysis.

Over the period 1925-1935 when she was writing for the *Occult Review,* Dion Fortune's interpretations of occult phenomena appear more and more in psychophysiological rather than purely psychological terms. She hypothesized a relationship between the chakras of occult philosophy's "etheric body" and the endocrine glands hormonal secretions in the human organism. She knew also that the endocrine system is controlled in the brain, and she was probably aware of the early experimental studies of the brain and the correlation of electrical activity of the human brain and human emotion.[14] Her conclusions on these subjects were

---

[14] The work of W. B. Cannon, P. Bard, W. E. Blatz, Franz Lashley, and others in the United States, including early experiments in electroencephalography and the galvanic skin response.

anything but final. She realized that not enough was known at the time to form more than tentative hypotheses, and she said so honestly.

Bernard Bromage had this to say in his article in *Light*, the Spiritualist journal quoted previously in this book:

> Dion Fortune never ceased to impress on me that she considered psychology to be the operative word. She herself, she said, had attained the greater part of her knowledge of magical techniques solely by a study of psychological principles.[15]

Bromage, in commenting on Dion Fortune's interest in Spiritualism said that this interest was largely due to the presence of psychic researchers in the field. "I cannot imagine her," he says, "without her 'psychological' background, her insistence on tangible validity and proof." The original purpose of the Fraternity of the Inner Light, he says, was to explore the boundaries between occultism and science.

Furthermore, Dion had a self-directed motivation to help others, especially those involved in unusual psychological obsessions and pathologies. I believe she would not have been afraid to confront Satan himself in order to save someone's soul. If only we still had the benefit of her courage and objectivity today. She saw magic and psychology as intimately related parts of one thing, and she was afraid of neither. She could truly live in the world but not be of it.

Dion's relationship with Crowley, the facts of her later years, and her position with regard to psychology are important elements in the synthesis of her personality and lifework. Several ideas raised in my conversation with Kenneth Grant on that day back in 1974 appeared again as I continued my research. I certainly hope that I have contributed some additional facts and some coherence to the whole story.

---

[15] Bernard Bromage, "Dion Fortune," *Light* (Spring, 1960), p. 4.

Chapter 9

VIOLET FIRTH'S PSYCHIC ATTACK: THE MYSTERY SOLVED

When I got back to the United States, the first thing I did was follow up on the references I had gotten from Mrs. Heathfield and Mr. Grant. That is, I wrote to all of the people whose names and addresses they had given to me.[1] Most of all I was interested in following up on the leads that would confirm or deny the theory that Studley Agricultural College was the place where Violet Firth suffered her psychic attack.

I am not reproducing the entirety of my correspondence on the subject of Dion Fortune's psychic attack because it is too lengthy and would, I feel, be tedious reading and of interest only to the scholar. What I am offering is my own hypothesis, a summary of the evidence, and my conclusion based on examination of the evidence. There is also the alternate opinion voiced by Mrs. Evelyn Heathfield based on the spirit message received through Hope Todd. The reader must draw his or her own conclusion.

I was fortunate in making contact with Elizabeth Hess, Principal of Studley from 1956 until 1969 when the college closed. She told me to write to the secretary of the Archives Department at the University of Reading for exact information regarding Dion Fortune's stay at Studley. The archivist wrote back confirming that the records of Studley College were deposited in their library. He

---

[1] Shortly after I returned to the United States, I received two letters from Christine Hartley (dated January 22, 1974, and March 22, 1974). Ms. Hartley said she would like to meet and added that she could provide additional information about Dion Fortune. I planned to return to England the following year, but the trip never materialized. I also received a letter dated May 31, 1975, from Iona Cammell, wife of Charles Cammell, author of *Aleister Crowley, The Man, The Mage, The Poet*. Mrs. Cammell told me that she met Dion Fortune only once and was not attracted to her. She did, however, provide some interesting information about Maiya Tranchell-Hayes.

also enclosed a "note," actually a detailed three-page report on the history of Studley College and specifically on Violet Firth's tenure there. I am exceedingly grateful to this anonymous person.

Studley College was founded in 1898 by Frances Evelyn, Countess of Warwick. In the Christmas issue of *The Land Magazine* for 1897, Lady Warwick outlined a plan for training women in the lighter aspects of agriculture. Her intent was to widen the available occupational opportunities for gentlewomen.

> My scheme was to train educated women in horticulture and agriculture. . . .It seemed to me that . . . dairy work, market gardening, poultry farming, bee-keeping, fruit growing, horticulture, and the grading, packing and marketing of produce, would appeal to many women of education, and would do something to meet the complaint that foreign competition was proving too much for our market gardeners.

Her decision was made at an opportune time because horticulture and agriculture were beginning to attract notice from several segments of society. The Royal Horticulture Society, founded in 1804 to improve the practice of horticulture, was, by the turn of the century, at the height of its prestige. At a banquet in the Hotel Metropole in the stifling July heat of 1899, members of the society met with distinguished foreign guests at the International Conference on Hybridization to discuss the rapidly accumulating data on genetics. In 1900 Mendel's paper on the segregation of characters was published in the society's *Journal,* and the greatly improved varieties of plants resulting from application of this theory were causing a virtual renaissance in the world of horticulture.

At the same time, improved conditions of transport were bringing caseloads of exotic plants to gardeners eager to transplant them in English soil. From China came magnolias and camellias, begonias from Bolivia and Peru, and rhododendrons from Java, Malaya, western China, and the Himalayas. The magnificent Lilium Auratum, the Golden-Rayed Lily, which had been introduced in 1860 from Japan, flowered in 1862, and when exhibited before the society it caused a sensation in the horticultural world. Before 1900 several species had been imported and were growing in England, causing a popular craze for lilies.

Figure 8. Studley Castle, Warwickshire. Drawing by Evelyn Fawcett Heathfield, February 22, 1974.

Meanwhile, the rural exodus and the increasing dependence on foreign imports were destroying the self-concept of educated English people and a nostalgia for the simple and the homemade began to haunt them. Running from the frightening images evoked by the decadence of their culture, the people strove to create a new, clearer world. The Horticultural Society responded to this sentiment and, with the object of obtaining a homegrown food supply, began sending representatives to local exhibitions, set up horticultural colleges, and gave examinations.

Demand for trained gardeners was still exceeding the supply, however, when Swanley Horticultural College opened its doors to women in the 1890s and the idea of women becoming gardeners began catching on. Now daughters of professional men, landowners, and the nobility would be given practical training in the growing and marketing of farm products, after which they would go "on the land" to bring about a closer and more efficient cooperation between the farmer, gardener, and consumer.

In August of 1898, Lady Warwick rented a large house in Bath Road, Reading, which by October 6 was ready to admit women for training in agriculture and horticulture in association with Reading College. Miss Edith Bradley was appointed principal, or "warden," of the school, which came to be called Lady Warwick Hostel. By 1901 the countess's innovation was receiving some publicity on the Continent, and curious visitors were coming from Canada and America. Locally it was often ridiculed as a "rich woman's fad," but there was a continuous demand for the trained students.

In July 1902 they severed their connection with Reading College, providing their own classes and lectures, and soon began to receive so many applications it became obvious they had to find larger quarters if they wished to grow. After an unsuccessful letter to the *Times* asking for an endowment, Lady Warwick turned to her husband and persuaded him to buy Studley Castle (see Figure 8, p. 163) and its 340 acre grounds in Warwickshire for £25,000. In December 1903 they moved in:

> The great adventure took much organization and money to launch, but from the start it was a success. We turned the old stables into dairies, cheese rooms, store rooms, etc., and the large hall of the Castle was used for lectures and demonstrations. In a short time the whole place was buzzing with young enthusiasts.[2]

For several years the college thrived on this fortuitous combination of youth, idealism, and the Warwick fortune, but unfortunately Lady Warwick's other interests began to consume more and more of her time, attention, and resources until finally, in 1908, because of mounting personal debts, she was unable to continue her support of the school. Miss Mabel Faithfull, who was warden of the college at this time, left when Lady Warwick did, and soon after the entire governing committee and several staff members also resigned. It was during this period of organizational and financial instability that Dr. Lillias Hamilton assumed control of the school, turning it into a semi-nursing home for neurotic young girls.

---

[2] F. Warwick, *Life's Ebb and Flow* (New York: William Morrow, 1929), p. 297-298.

Evelyn Heathfield gave me a vivid picture of life at Studley College during this period as well as a precious glimpse of her classmate, the young Violet Firth:

> We used to go up to work, every morning, up a long cinder path, which led from the college up to the gardens. And on my first morning there, being very raw, very young—I was only eighteen and very . . . a slow developer—but as I walked up, feeling rather lost and rather lonely, I was overtaken by somebody who walked in beside me, and she said, "Oh, my name is Firth." I said, "My name is Fawcett." We wore navy blue skirts, which had to be eight inches off the ground and which was considered terribly short in those days, and a sax apron with two pockets in the front, a white shirt blouse, and the college tie. I can see her. She overtook me, and she looked down at me with a sort of smile, and to this *day* I can't remember, but I think she had a tooth missing. It was a crooked smile. She said: "Oh, are you mad? Or don't you get on at home? Or have you been crossed in love?"
>
> And I said, "But I—I don't think I'm any of those things! I've come here to be a gardener!"[3]

The students had to be at practical work in the gardens by 9:00 A.M. They went by the cinder path from the forecourt of the house to the utility gardens, across a grass field. Some ambitious workers would be there already, using the extra time to work their own private patches of ground. On one side were the greenhouses and on the other a vinery and "French Garden" where vegetables were "forced." There was a large, walled kitchen garden, some peach houses and ornamental plant houses, and an orchard. At the end was the potting shed where the girls signed on for work.

From the top of the hill spread out the 40 acres of gardens, 250 acres of farmland, and beyond that, woodlands. Behind the castle, the south lawn sloped down to a meadow and an artificial

---

[3] Evelyn Heathfield from an interview with the author, January 8, 1974.

lake. To the west the old stables were hidden by trees, and the long drive from the road was bordered in spring and summer by an avenue of Wellingtonias. There was a rose garden, an abandoned orangery, and a "wild garden" of trees. Hidden in the middle of this was "Neptune's Garden" containing only a statue of the god and a long since empty pool.[4]

Most of the teaching consisted of demonstrations in the garden or greenhouse. A head man, master in his special field, would perform an operation for a group of first-year students, explaining what he was doing and why. This observation period would be followed by the students' own awkward trials under the advice, criticism, and encouragement of the specialist. The girls had to develop the ability to mimic the master's gestures until, with practice, they became natural and automatic.

For the experienced students, the daily work was a succession of physical motions, involving the whole body, but especially the arms and hands, each action dependent on the preceding one, and all necessary for the particular goal desired. The aim was always to get the most from the least amount of effort, and one result of this was that everything was put to some use.

Cleanliness and order were unspoken rules. The ultimate goal, "a homegrown food supply," was also kept in mind—or was supposed to be—and "weekly lectures on business method followed by bookkeeping classes" prepared the girls for the day when they would go out and manage their own farms and market gardens.[5]

Occasionally, a girl would become deeply involved with one group of plants or animals, tending to them with a mother's vigilance. When this resulted in the girl becoming an expert in her particular area, she could rise to the role of head student and would be allowed to give instruction; sometimes a girl who had finished her student training would be invited to stay on at the school as a member of the staff. Violet, whose special interest was breeding

---

[4] Ibid.
[5] Information on curriculum from *Life's Ebb and Flow*, pp. 299-302; and from Viscountess Wolseley, *In a College Garden* (New York: Charles Scribner's Sons, 1917), p. 20.

and raising domestic birds, was offered the position of Head of the Poultry Department after completing a two-year course.

At this time, the college had been keeping white leghorn fowl for eight years. They were judged the most profitable investment because they ate less grain and produced more eggs than other breeds. They were hatched in April or May, grew up fast and healthy in the spring and summer weather, and were ready to lay by October. The newborn chicks had to be fed every two hours and required elaborate and sensitive supervision:

> We hatch them under a barn-door fowl and feed them for the first week entirely on small chicko, with a little chopped meat after they are two days old. Next they receive the large chicko and some soft food, such as biscuit meal. Later they get fewer meals and the adults have only two in the day.[6]

What Violet was getting for her efforts at Studley was a feeling for how life processes can be influenced by conscious control of heredity and environment. For example, one practice to which she was undoubtedly exposed was Thomas Andrew Knight's idea of adapting the fruit to the soil. An early exponent of scientific horticulture, he had found that what is good for one variety of any species is not usually good for another. Violet was to use this principle later in life when training her students in the Fraternity of the Inner Light. She would consider each person's background and needs individually and would set up a specific program to maximize his or her unique potential. Her careful selection, training, and polarization of the Inner Light students eventually produced several outstanding individuals.

But there was another, fun-loving, side to her nature, and this too revealed itself in her college days. Although she was remembered by more than one fellow student as being rather shy, Violet was well-known at Studley for her keen sense of humor, which was frequently expressed in "kindly practical joking."[7] It was

---

[6] *News About the Guild: Being the Magazine of the Guild of the Daughters of Ceres*, Vol. 5, No. 1 (February, 1913), p. 61. (From 1909 until 1945 this quarterly journal reported on activities at Studley College.)

[7] Evelyn Heathfield.

known that the warden left a mug beside her bed at night and it was whispered among the girls that it was not her teeth that she kept in it, but her eye. In the summer the girls took their mattresses and slept out of doors and one morning Violet, having woken up early, was making her way back to the college to get dressed. She had to pass the gate to the "Warden's Garden," a hedged off piece of ground outside the warden's room, where the warden was also "sleeping out" with the mug beside her. Vi was seized with a sudden devilish urge to find out for herself exactly what was in the mug, and creeping across the lawn, she peeked into the cup, finding, of course, a set of false teeth. With her curiosity satisfied, she was about to go on her way, when she saw the warden's eye looking at her. She was startled but instead of running she said, "Good morning, Warden" and the warden answered, "Good morning, Miss Firth," after which Violet walked away. Schoolgirls did not usually escape so easily. Violet obeyed rules, but she was not in awe of authority and so was not easily cowed. Incidents such as these, however, did not help endear her to the warden.

As she began to settle into college life, however, Violet discovered a more constructive outlet for her playfulness in writing and producing satirical playlets about the school. Two of these plays were produced in 1912 and 1913 for the biggest social event of the school year, February 7, the warden's birthday. There was often a full holiday from work, a hockey match, and in the evening the girls would assemble in the Round Hall for refreshments and entertainment. On February 7, 1912, it was a play called "Now and Then, a Contrast" by N. Brunton and V. Firth:

> In the first act, Studley Castle in 1812 was shown, "when women sewed" and were horrified at anything not proper, but one of the daughters of the house dreamt what Studley would be in 100 years' time. In Act II, "when women sowed," 14 students of Studley College gathered in the Round Hall . . . to relate the varied experiences of the present inhabitants of the Castle.

After the performance, the warden surprised the girls with supper in the Drawing Room; then there was dancing in the Common Room, "and so ended an evening we believe all enjoyed." The following year, only three months before her final, disastrous encounter with the woman, Violet had another play ready for Dr. Hamilton's birthday, this time in collaboration with a Miss Pearson. The play "Babes in the Castle" was a pantomime caricaturing members of the staff and the student body and was a huge success.[8]

Violet's promotion to the staff in January of 1913 gave her an inside view of the warden's administration. A rapid series of breakdowns, changes, and dismissals had been occurring. The warden, bristling with plans for reorganizing the entire school, couldn't be bothered with giving a term's notice to people who stood in her way. Eleven men, three boys, and four women had been fired in five weeks, and there were still "some unsatisfactory people to replace."[9]

At the first staff meeting of the year, the warden had instituted a new policy. Henceforth, "the line between senior and junior" would be "less firmly drawn" and the new labels "competent" and "incompetent" would be substituted: "Woe be to the senior who, after being weighed in the balance, is found to have no sense of responsibility—there will be nothing for her, but to give up her place to a more competent junior!" Under the guise of being "an incentive to good work,"[10] this tactic had really been another of the warden's means of achieving her personal desires by making puppets of her subordinates.

But Violet had only begun to understand what was going on when she had found herself involved in a succession of vicious intrigues. At first, she had been forced into giving evidence damaging to the reputation of certain staff members that the warden wanted to get rid of. Next, she discovered that the warden was attempting to persuade a wealthy student, an orphan, to place her money at her disposal. When this scheme backfired—the trustees of the girl's estate having removed her bodily from the school—the identical plot was replayed with a new victim, this time old "Auntie Barclay," a mentally retarded woman, "plain and rather

---

[8] *News About the Guild*, Vol. 4, No. 1 (February, 1912), p. 8; and Vol. 5, No. 1 (February, 1913), p. 61.

[9] *News About the Guild*, Vol. 5, No. 1 (February, 1913), p. 58.

[10] *News About the Guild*, Vol. 5, No. 1 (February, 1913), p. 59.

odd looking but with a sense of humour and a huge smile."[11] But Violet was no longer an innocent child, and unwilling to stand by and "see old 'Auntie' rooked,"[12] she packed her off to relatives while the warden was temporarily away.

Not much time elapsed, however, before the warden found out who had helped "Auntie," and it was then that Violet realized she had better pack up and leave as soon as possible, because if she didn't go of her own accord she would probably suffer at least dismissal, and possibly attacks on her character that would make it difficult for her to secure a position elsewhere.

Dr. Lillias Hamilton, the hated and respected Warden of Studley College, was, in spite of her "unreasonable outbursts of anger," a woman of great charm, fascinating to watch and talk about. She "invariably wore long dresses hanging shapeless from the shoulders with a round neck and loose sleeves." Her hair, "the cause of much ribald speculation,"[13] was pulled to a bun at the top of her head, and around this she wore a wig of "tight ginger brown curls." Her appearance, combined with rumors of her residence in India, conjured mysterious "oriental" associations in the impressionable minds of her young students.

Dr. Hamilton had received her M.D. from the University of Edinburgh at a time when the practice of medicine was just opening to women. It was a long and difficult apprenticeship for which theoretical knowledge was not enough. All the students, women as well as men, spent time in a hospital or clinic learning "to manage people." A medical woman was taught to be "brave, firm, self-controlled and a devotee of duty"; she was expected to "reason correctly, to act promptly, and to acquire influence over her subordinates and patients."[14]

Brilliant and ambitious, Dr. Hamilton readily developed these abilities, but, unfortunately, without any real feelings of empathy, which were essential for the difficult mission she had selected. She

---

[11] Evelyn Heathfield in a personal letter dated February 26, 1974.

[12] Dion Fortune, Psychic Self-Defense, pp. 12-13.

[13] Evelyn Heathfield in a personal letter dated February 26, 1974.

[14] Frances Warwick, ed. *Progress in Women's Education in the British Empire* (London: Longmans Green, 1898), pp. 94, 102.

chose to work among the women of India who were known for their ability to sense a person's real sympathies and who were quick to notice any slight. Nevertheless, what she lacked in sympathy she made up for in determination, eventually becoming head of the Women's Hospital in Calcutta. At this point in her career, perhaps she should have stopped, but the Emir of Afganistan asked her to become his personal physician. The role was so alluring she overlooked questions of tact and accepted. Conversation with him was evidently worth any risk, since "the jealousy of the Ameer's wives and their annoyance at a Western woman being in personal contact with their lord was so great, that Dr. Hamilton was in constant danger of her life. For safety's sake, everything she ate and drank was tested by a special food taster appointed by the Ameer."[15] The British government refused to get involved on her behalf, and she eventually had difficulty escaping.

As I have mentioned before, I am grateful to the archivist at the University of Reading for his report on Studley College. This report, as well as the copies of *News About the Guild* he sent to me, provided most of the above information.

For those who still need more proof that Violet Firth did in fact attend Studley College, I now quote a portion of the archivist's report:

> The Archives as such of Studley College give no information. As you will see from the historical note about the college which I enclose, it was privately owned and supported until 1912. The surviving records for that period are very patchy. Records of students (or even of staff) simply do not exist, even for the later years.
>
> Nevertheless, there are references to Miss Firth in various issues of *News about the Guild: Being the magazine of the Guild of the Daughters of Ceres*. This journal, a quarterly, though not published by the College, gives notes about its activities from 1909 until 1945. Miss Firth first appears in the issue for February 1912 as part-author of a play presented to mark the Warden's birthday. Since

---

[15] F. Warwick, *Life's Ebb and Flow*, p. 301.

the play deals with both Studley College and the Castle, one can fairly assume that Miss Firth had been a student there for some time previously. The College year seems to have started in January with the Spring Term, which lasted until April. The Summer Term followed from May until about July; the Autumn Term, beginning in September, lasted until Christmas. Students appear to have followed courses for at least one year, sometimes two or even three, depending on the standard they wished to reach. Some courses, e.g., in Beekeeping, lasted only a few months. Miss Firth, as you will see from the issue of *News about the Guild* for February 1913, actually joined the teaching staff in that year, which suggests that she took her studies to a fairly advanced level. Though the magazine gives no definite evidence, I think we can assume that she had been at the College since at least the beginning of 1911 on a two year course including poultry management. She was employed as an Assistant in the Poultry Department until the end of the Spring Term 1913 (see *News about the Guild*, May 1913). To give a specific answer to Mrs. James' enquiry, therefore, we can say with reasonable certainty that Miss Firth attended Studley College as a student from January 1911 until December 1912 and as a member of staff from January 1913 until April 1913.

I needn't retell word-for-word Dr. Hamilton's psychic attack on the young Violet. Dion Fortune tells this story herself in *Psychic Self-Defense*.[16] Undoubtedly, Dr. Hamilton saw Violet as a trouble-maker and decided to use one of the techniques she had learned in India to keep Violet from leaving the school. Fear of a scandal or, at best, bad publicity were Dr. Hamilton's motives for attacking the girl.

"Very well, if you want to go, go you shall. But before you go you have got to admit that you are incompetent and have no self-confidence."

---

[16] The author's account of this incident, dialogue, and all direct quotations come from *Psychic Self-Defense*, pp. 14-16.

To this Violet replied, "If I am incompetent, why don't you dismiss me yourself?" Then added spitefully that she was "the product of her own training school."

Barely ruffled, the warden repeated: "You are incompetent and you know it. You have no self-confidence, and you have got to admit it."

"That is not true. I know my work, and you know I know it."

But for the third time: "You are incompetent, and you know it. You have no self-confidence, and you have got to admit it."

"That is not true. I know my work, and you know I know it."

And again: "You are incompetent, and you know it. You have no self-confidence, . . ."

Minutes became hours. Meaning disappeared in a stream of endless repetition. The room pulsed to the slow, relentless chant, and the girl's strength waned under the power of the old woman. As Violet's vitality reached its lowest ebb, and when her sense of reality had receded almost to the borders of panic, a change occurred in her consciousness, and she heard a voice from within her brain, insistent, distinct: "Pretend you are beaten before you really are. Then she will let up the attack and you will be able to get away." Violet obeyed the voice. She apologized to the warden and promised to return to her duties, under the mistaken impression that she was fooling her.

Dr. Hamilton knew better. Successfully hypnotized subjects always think they are only pretending to comply in order to please the hypnotist. In reality, Dr. Hamilton had gotten exactly what she wanted. The girl's will was broken now, and as far as leaving was concerned, well, the poor thing could hardly stand up; in fact, there she was on the floor, actually kneeling before her. Yes, she was "well satisfied with the morning's work" and could dismiss the repentant Miss Firth to be dealt with later, at her leisure.

Safe, momentarily, from the warden's eyes, but too weak to make any further efforts to escape, Violet managed to get to her room where she collapsed unconscious on her bed. Thirty hours later she was accidentally discovered by the housekeeper, who revived her with cold water and a good shaking. Still too disoriented to leave, however, she remained in her room trying to collect her thoughts. Three days of this confusion had passed before a concerned friend came in search of her, alarmed to find Violet lying on the bed with "dry mouth, sweating palms, thumping heart and shallow, hasty breathing."

Dr. Hamilton was embarrassed by the sudden arrival of Violet's parents. They were "extremely suspicious" and made Dr. Hamilton "exceedingly uncomfortable." After all, they had sent their daughter there to recover from a nervous illness, and now she was obviously much worse. Unfortunately, this very fact made it all the more difficult for them to accuse the warden of any specific wrongdoing because she could always say that Violet had never completely recovered from the illness she had had before coming to Studley, and that she was suffering a relapse from overwork. A short notice in the "College Notes" for May 1913 said: "Miss Dupree is no longer housekeeper, though still at the College in another capacity, and Miss Firth has left the Poultry Department."[17]

Evidently Dr. Hamilton was capable, intelligent, ambitious, at times eccentric, and always intimidating. In a letter postmarked February 26, 1974, Evelyn Heathfield sent me the following description of her:

> *Dr. Hamilton*: A very interesting woman—M.D. of Edinburgh, with a brilliant mind. Had spend some years in the Far East, privately employed to doctor an Eastern potentate I believe in Afganistan, but I don't know, and the females in his harem. The British government refused to be responsible for her so she went at her own risk and eventually had some difficulty in escaping! A woman of great charm when she liked but given to unreasonable outbursts of anger. She invariably wore long dresses hanging shapeless from the shoulders with a round neck and loose sleeves and a shirt blouse under it. We called it a *dgibba*. I do not know the spelling and have never heard the word since! Her hair was the cause of much ribald speculation. It was pulled tight to the crown of the head and finished in a small tight knob. Over this was a wig of tight ginger brown curls and the knob stuck

---

[17] *News About the Guild*, Vol. 5, No. 2 (May, 1913), p. 71.

through a hole in the wig. It was commonly believed that her hairdressing consisted of removing the wig and hanging it over the bedpost at night.

The next two excerpts are from letters written by former students at Studley College. While neither Miss Rotherham nor Mrs. Tuck remembers Violet, both have distinct recollections of Dr. Hamilton. Margaret Rotherham, however, was reluctant to say too much:

> Dr. Hamilton had such an interesting and complex character that it would not be fair to ask anyone who did not know her well, to write about her, and I cannot think of anyone now alive who could give you a true story.
>
> Personally I always got on very well with her and I think she liked me but I could not commit to paper all I feel—and whatever one wrote I feel it could be a contradiction. I only wish that someone who knew her well had written her life.

Mrs. W. H. Tuck, who wrote to me from Maryland, referred to her as "our admired and feared Dr. Lillias Hamilton."

> I was only the year in Studley. My sister was 2 years and a great favorite of the Warden. Doctor Hamilton came to my wedding in 1920 and came to stay with us in Brussels. She often talked of her time in Afganistan when Queen Victoria ordered her to return to England. . . . As she was not strong she stayed often in bed and gave her orders through a window which gave on her private garden. She had an overwhelming strong character and frightened me very much especially as she painted my sister as being so superior! . . . Although she thought very little of me she often took me on her motorcycle. Thanks to that I saw a great deal of the countryside which I loved. But I was very scared of our rides.

Following are quotations from *News About the Guild*. Dr. Hamilton herself is talking here about her recent reorganization of the school. It is suggested that the reader compare Dr. Hamilton's statements with pages 12–13 in *Psychic Self-Defense*.

The change on the agricultural side is not quite so radical because there are still unsatisfactory people to replace there and some, I am thankful to say, were satisfactory and remain but I have to announce with much regret that Summers and Lawrence have gone. Lawrence left once before, when the old Committee resigned in 1909. He felt the place must go under without the old hands at the helm and he did not want to be here, when the ship sank. The same reason has made him resign again! He is by nature very conservative, with certain socialistic tendencies, imbibed from Rochester, I should think. West reigns in his stead. I hope he may soon find work, where he will be as much appreciated, as he was here, but I doubt it. The fact is, that every year, the number of competent helmsmen and helmswomen increases, so that a change, even as radical a one as there has been this Christmas, causes less anxiety than the changes that took place in 1909 and 1910, when I knew less well, where to put my hand on competent men, and when there were fewer competent women to come to my aid.

On the next page, she goes on to discuss the students:

Where we had only one real teacher in the gardens we now have three and every capable student is, in her own little department, a demonstrator of the work in which she has been previously instructed and in which she has even had some experience, she herself becoming a student pure and simple when the work in her house, or portion of the garden, permit of her working in another department. Thus, the vine student in charge, is a pupil in the rose garden, and the rose-garden student is a pupil in the carnation house, and so on. The line between senior and junior is to be less and less firmly drawn and is really to exist rather between "competent and incompetent." This without any reflection on the newcomers, who are of course "uninstructed," but who may now speedily be given a charge if it seems wise in their own interests and those of their fellow students. This should

be an incentive to good work from the very start, and
woe be to the senior who, after being weighed in the balance, is found to have no sense of responsibility—there
will be nothing for her, but to give up her place to a more
competent junior!

And, lastly, the following:

Before I close I must say a word about Mr. Hope, who
came to my assistance for five weeks, and without
whom, it seems to me, it would have been impossible
to have steered our ship into safety. It is a very serious
thing in an Educational establishment to have the actual
Heads of every department new at the same moment,
and not only the Heads but those immediately under
them, too. We have had to replace 11 men, 3 boys and 4
women, in five weeks, and settle these into their proper
niches. I am sure anyone will agree with me, that to do
this successfully was more than one person's work.

I would like to call attention to the warden's preference for the
terms *competent* and *incompetent*, to her general tone, and to the
actual events that are described. I have compared Dion's account
in *Psychic Self-Defense* with the account quoted above, which was,
as I said previously, written by Dr. Hamilton herself. I found the
two accounts to fit exactly regarding the chronology of events, the
nature of the events themselves, and the descriptions of the personalities involved.

Of further interest is evidence that Violet had come to Studley
in the first place because of a prior breakdown. All indications are
that Violet was a hypersensitive child, shy and yet with a keen
interest in dramatics and practical joking—her way of getting attention and expressing her rich creative abilities. She was one of many
nervous breakdown cases Dr. Hamilton had taken in during the
period after the Countess of Warwick had withdrawn her support
of the school and before they began to get annual grants from the
Ministry of Agriculture. "Those were the days when the dreaded
'anemia' had so many easy victims among girls," the countess had
put it. "Studley gave the girls a new outlook, and a few months

of healthy outdoor work, spreading manure, or attending to the cart horses or taking a turn at the dairy, made new creatures of them."[18]

In all fairness to Dr. Hamilton, I must repeat that Violet was not in perfect mental health when she came to Studley in 1911. At school she was a prankster and perhaps in her first year somewhat of a troublemaker as well. But in view of the evidence, there can be no doubt that Dr. Hamilton was unscrupulous, that the interview did occur, and that when Dion Fortune in *Psychic Self-Defense* speaks of "the training college" or "educational establishment" she is speaking of Studley, and when she says "the Warden" she is referring to Dr. Hamilton. *Psychic Self-Defense* must be considered as autobiography. Only the names are omitted. Moreover, the incidents she relates are used as illustrations for her central thesis; if they are untrue, then the whole book falls with them. A careful reading of the first page of her preface should convince anyone that she is speaking the truth.

As I have explained previously, my conclusions are not based on *Psychic Self-Defense* alone but on careful study of the papers deposited in the University of Reading by the Trustees of Studley College in 1969 when the college was closed, as well as on personal interviews with Studley alumnae from the period 1911-1913.

The actions of Dr. Hamilton should in no way reflect on the good name of the college or its graduates. Dr. Hamilton was hired during a period of instability and transition, and it is possible she secured her position by exercising undue influence on the impressionable Lady Warwick herself.

As far as Evelyn Heathfield's insistence that Dion's psychic attack did not occur at Studley, there is no evidence to support this theory except for the spirit messages received from Hope Todd. If the attack did not occur at Studley, why did Dion Fortune give dates of events that could eventually implicate Dr. Hamilton? If the attack did not occur there, why did Dion say she had entered the educational establishment at 20, the exact age at which she entered Studley? Given the perfect fit between the warden described by Dion, and the warden described by Mrs. Heathfield

---

[18] F. Warwick, *Life's Ebb and Flow*, pp. 301-302.

and other students at Studley, as well as the warden described by Lady Warwick and the warden whose personality comes through so well in her own writing, is it possible that another warden existed at some prior educational establishment Dion had attended and *that* warden was exactly like Dr. Hamilton in personality and behavior? And wouldn't it have to have been an even stranger coincidence that the identical events occurred at both places?

It is my opinion that Evelyn Heathfield, like the other former Studley students who wrote to me, wanted to protect the image of the school. Perhaps the eye of the warden was still staring at them from the grave.

Now that these previously unknown portions of Dion Fortune's life are more clear to us, we can say with conviction that Violet's stay at Studley College strongly influenced her in several ways. To begin with, she learned the latest information in the field of genetics, particularly Thomas Andrew Knight's idea of "adapting the fruit to the soil." As was noted earlier, Dion employed this concept when developing the curriculim for the Inner Light study courses. Studley also gave her ample outlet for her dramatic abilities. We can easily imagine the young Violet directing her own plays in the Great Hall of Studley Castle. And we can recognize in that young girl the talented personality who would later become an expert in the field of ritual magic.

At Studley, Violet also came under the personal influence of the warden. Later, as Dion Fortune, she was to become a warden herself, that is, Warden of the Fraternity of the Inner Light. I would go so far as to say that Dion consciously or unconsciously, imitated the warden when she came to head her own group. Not that she imitated Dr. Hamilton's sinister ways—Dion was a kind and benevolent leader—but Dr. Hamilton's magnetic personality, her aura of mystery, her flamboyant style of dress; these, I feel, were, perhaps without conscious intention, adopted by Dion Fortune. After all, everyone who knew Dr. Lillias Hamilton had both good and bad to say about her. I think Violet Firth emulated Dr. Hamilton's strengths as much as she was both frightened and fascinated by her weaknesses.

When, in later years, Violet would take up her pen as "Dion Fortune" to write *Psychic Self-Defense*, she would, using no names, base her conclusions on her own experiences in the first months

of 1913 under Dr. Lillias Hamilton, the Warden of Studley
Horticultural College. By that time she would be 38, head of her
own school, and the trauma would be only a painful memory, necessary to recall and relate so that others might be on their guard
against similar persons. Normally, Dion Fortune avoided direct
reference to herself, preferring to conceal the facts of her history
behind the characters in her novels. But in this case, she obviously
felt she had no choice but to tell the truth, because without the
support of firsthand experience, her theory of psychic attack and
defense would lack credibility. Consequently, in her preface to
Psychic Self-Defense, we have one of the rare instances in which
Dion Fortune wrote autobiographically:

> I cite my own case, painful as it is to me to do so, because
> an ounce of experience is worth a pound of theory. It
> was this experience which led me to take up the study of
> analytical psychology, and subsequently of occultism.
>
> As soon as I touched the deeper aspects of practical
> psychology and watched the dissection of the mind
> under psycho-analysis, I realised that there was very
> much more in the mind than was accounted for by
> accepted psychological theories. I saw that we stood in
> the centre of a small circle of light thrown by accurate
> scientific knowledge, but around us was a vast, circum-
> ambient sphere of darkness, and in that darkness dim
> shapes were moving.

Epilogue

In December of 1974 I had an experience that caused me to walk away from my study of occult and magical subjects. The experience happened in connection with the Golden Dawn system of initiation, which I was following on my own. I experienced an almost total disintegration of personality as well as the destruction of most of the structures of my personal and public life. I now know that this can happen when you study serious subjects without a teacher, but I was a long time recovering, and when I did I was no longer the same person I had been.

It wasn't until September of 1989 when I paid my first visit to The Glastonbury Bookshop in Tallahassee, Florida, where I now live, that the threads of my past life as an occultist began to weave themselves into a new magical garment. Len Schweitzer, owner of the bookshop, a kind and ebullient wizard of a man, clued me in to recent developments in my particular specialty. He ordered *Priestess* for me and *Dancers to the Gods.* I began reassembling my collection of occult literature, the central part of which was new paperback editions of Dion Fortune's works.

Several things troubled me about *Priestess,* not the least of which was the knowledge that I had once accumulated a wealth of material pertaining to two important aspects of Dion's life that Richardson had no information about. Suddenly I was seized with the desire to write the book on Dion Fortune I had always wanted to write.

Fortunately, my research materials, tapes, correspondence, and photographs had been saved for me by a friend. At my request, she packed everything into a box and mailed it to me. When I read over my old notes and the letters from people who had known Dion Fortune, the whole world I had once been in surrounded me again. I began working on the book and gradually *Quest for Dion Fortune* took shape.

I hope that my book has filled in some gaps in this extraordinary woman's story and that it has put some opinions about her into perspective. It is important to realize, for example, that Dion Fortune had a sincere interest in and respect for the "hard" sciences—physics, biology, chemistry, mathematics. Although she usually carried the facts further than most scientists would have, she *knew* the facts nevertheless. Although she maintained her belief that the endocrine glands were controlled by the "emotions," had she lived longer she probably would have learned that emotions are physiological phenomena generated by the human brain in concert with the rest of the physical organism. Perhaps then she would have postulated a higher seat of governance in some astral realm.

The point is, she didn't shy away from natural laws and she didn't perceive these laws as in opposition to those of occult philosophy. Dion's understanding of science affected a significant change in the current of contemporary occult thought. She was like the Greek philosopher/mathematician, Pythagoras. Pythagoras was also respected as a religious teacher who taught a mystical and metaphysical view of reality not in contradiction with his scientific discoveries. Pythagoras' belief in the divine nature of reality was in no way inconsistent with his understanding of mathematics. In fact, his discovery of the mathematical basis of musical intervals led him to speculate that the universe itself was designed along harmonic principles. His reverence for the natural in no way inhibited his moral sense or his religious procilivities. So it was with D. F.

As science progressed, and as the language of science became increasingly difficult to understand, scientists and occultists split into enemy camps. Scientists challenged occultists to prove the secrets of life they claimed to have in their possession. This challenge caused many occultists to feel that their private world was being invaded. Their only defense was to say that reality intuitively perceived was better than the world seen through the lens of logic, and that reality could never be subjected to scientific analysis. Undaunted, the scientist turned his method and instruments upon the mind itself.

Then came the Industrial Revolution and the theory of natural selection. Philosophers and theologians became painfully aware that if they didn't take into account the discoveries of science, their theories about the nature of humanity and the universe would become obsolete.

Today, science is still concerned with some of the same fundamentals that preoccupy the occultist: the origin and destiny of the universe and humanity's function in it, the nature of perception and consciousness, the working of the brain, and the question, "Do we have a will?" The occultist should be aware of the currents of thought in humanistic psychology, phenomenology, the study of altered states of consciousness psychology, neuroscience and related fields. But we must be careful not to look simply for justification of our own theories.

With a clear understanding of the nature and operation of magic, its powers and limitations, and a willingness to learn from other disciplines, the occultist can come out of hiding and take on the challenges posed by other viewpoints.

Let us not forget the groundwork laid by Dion Fortune that enables occult science to enter the New Age. She was a pioneer, and a philosopher in the original sense of the word, i.e., a seeker after truth. She was also a sane, well-integrated personality, dedicated to a high ideal of human responsibility and conduct, to individual purification of character, and to completion of the Great Work.

When I want to picture Dion Fortune in my mind, I call up her marriage photograph, the one in which she is enlarged and Penry Evans is "out of the picture." And I think of Bernard Bromage's description:

> She had the posture of some elected oracle proclaiming
> the Unescapable Law. . . . She was a striking figure. . . .
> Her rather plump figure was swathed in a crimson gown
> of hieratic cut; on her head she wore a black, flapping
> hat. There was an odd atmosphere about her of the sibyl,
> the prophetess, the diver into deep occult seas.

May her courage to investigate the darker aspects of the subconscious mind teach us never to be idle or cowardly in our fight against evil. May her concern for the welfare of her friends and followers remind us of her devotion to the Master Jesus. And may her Light continue to guide other seekers toward the Right-Hand Path.

Selected Bibliography

Ackerman, Sandra. *Discovering the Brain*. Washington: Institute of Medicine, National Academy of Sciences, National Academy Press, 1992.

Ashe, Geoffrey. *King Arthur's Avalon: The Story of Glastonbury*. New York: Dutton, 1958.

Avalon, Arthur. *The Serpent Power*. New York: Dover, 1974.

Aveling, Francis. *Directing Mental Energy*. New York: George H. Doran, 1927.

———. *Personality and Will*. New York: D. Appleton.

——— . *The Psychological Approach to Reality*. London: University of London Press, 1929.

Bond, Frederick Bligh. *The Gate of Remembrance*. Alexandria, VA: Time Life, 1990.

———. *Hill of Vision*. London: Constable, 1919.

Bromage, Bernard. "Dion Fortune." *Light*. (Spring, 1960).

Budge, E. Wallis. *Egyptian Book of the Dead: The Papyrus of Ani in the British Museum*. New York: Dover, 1967.

Burland, C. A. *The Magical Arts: A Short History*. New York: Horizon Press, 1966.

Butler, W. E. *Apprenticed to Magic*. London: Aquarian Press, 1981.

———. *Lords of Light: The Path of Initiation in the Western Mysteries*. Rochester, VT: Inner Traditions, 1990.

———. *Magic: Its Ritual Power and Purposes*. New York: Samuel Weiser, 1952.

————. *The Magician: His Training and Work*. Los Angeles: Wilshire, 1959.

Colquhoun, Ithell. *Sword of Wisdom: MacGregor Mathers and the Golden Dawn*. New York: G. P. Putnam Sons, 1975.

Crowley, Aleister. *The Book of the Law*. York Beach, ME: Samuel Weiser, 1976.

————. *Clouds without Water*, London: Privately published, 1909.

————. *Collected Works of Aleister Crowley*. London: Foyers Society for the Propagation of Religious Truth, 1905.

Eddy, Mary Baker. *Science and Health with Key to the Scriptures*. Boston: Trustees under the will of Mary Baker Eddy, 1934.

Encausse, Gérard (Papus). *Traité méthodique de science occulte*. Paris: Carré, 1891.

Fielding, Charles and Carr Collins. *The Story of Dion Fortune*. Dallas, TX: Star & Cross, 1985.

Fodor, Nardor. *Encyclopedia of Psychic Science*. New York: Carol Publishing Group, 1974.

Fortune, Dion (Violet Firth). *The Cosmic Doctrine*. York Beach, ME: Samuel Weiser, 1976.

————. "Ceremonial Magic Unveiled." *Occult Review* (January, 1933).

————. "The Death of Miss N. Fornario." *Occult Review* (January, 1930).

————. *The Demon Lover*. York Beach, ME: Samuel Weiser, 1972.

————. *Esoteric Orders and Their Work and the Training and Work of an Initiate*. London: Aquarian Press, 1987.

————. *The Esoteric Philosophy of Love and Marriage and the Problem of Purity*. London: Aquarian Press, 1988.

————. *Glastonbury: Avalon of the Heart*. London: Aquarian Press, 1989.

————. *The Machinery of the Mind*. York Beach, ME: Samuel Weiser, 1980.

————. *Moon Magic*. York Beach, ME: Samuel Weiser, 1979.

————. *The Mystical Qabalah*. York Beach, ME: Samuel Weiser, 1984.

————. *Psychic Self-Defense*. York Beach, ME: Samuel Weiser, 1991; London: Aquarian Press, 1957.

————. *Sane Occultism* and *Practical Occultism in Daily Life*. London: Aquarian Press, 1987.

————. *The Sea Priestess*. York Beach, ME: Samuel Weiser, 1987.

————. *The Secrets of Dr. Taverner*. Alpharetta, GA: Ariel Press, 1989.

————. *Through the Gates of Death* and *Spiritualism in the Light of Occult Sciences*. London: Aquarian Press, 1987.

————. *The Winged Bull*. York Beach, ME: Samuel Weiser, 1980.

Freud, Sigmund. *Beyond The Pleasure Principle*. New York: Norton, 1990; and London: Hogarth Press, 1957.

————. *New Introductory Letters on Psychoanalysis*. New York: W. W. Norton, 1933.

————. *On Dreams*. New York: W. W. Norton, 1963.

————. *Outline of Psychoanalysis*. New York: W. W. Norton, 1989.

Grant, Kenneth. *Aleister Crowley and the Hidden God*. London: Frederick Muller, 1973.

————. "Dion Fortune." *Man, Myth, and Magic* (Issue #36: Vol. 8: pp. 1021-1023) New York: Marshall Cavendish, 1970.

————. *The Magical Revival*. London: Skoob Books, 1991.

————. *Outside the Circles of Time*. London: Frederick Muller, 1980.

————. *Remembering Aleister Crowley*. London: Skoob Books, 1991.

Harth, Erich. *Dawn of a Millenium: Beyond Evolution and Culture*. Boston: Little Brown, 1990.

Hartley, Christine. *The Western Mystery Tradition*. London: Aquarian Press, 1986.

Howe, Ellic. *The Magicians of the Golden Dawn*. York Beach, ME: Samuel Weiser, 1978.

Jeannerod, Marc. *The Brain Machine: The Development of Neurophysiological Thought*. Cambridge, MA: Harvard University Press, 1985.

Jones, Ernest. *The Life and Work of Sigmund Freud* (3 Volumes). New York: Basic Books, 1974. See especially Volume 3, pp. 375-407.

Jung, Carl. *The Integration of the Personality*. New York & Toronto: Farrar & Rinehart, 1939.

————. *The Psychology of the Unconscious*. New York: Moffat, Yard and Company, 1916. Also, Princeton, NJ: Princeton University Press, 1966. Vol. 7 of the Collected Works.

King, Francis. *Ritual Magic in England*. Saffron Walden, England: Neville Spearman, 1970.

King, Walter John. *The British Isles*. London: Macdonald & Evans, 1970.

Levi, Eliphas. *The Key of the Mysteries*. York Beach, ME: Samuel Weiser, 1970.

Moriarty, Theodore. *The Seven Aphorisms of Creation*. London: Welbecson Press, n.d.

Myers, Frederic W. *Human Personality and Its Survival of Bodily Death* (2 Volumes). New York: Longmans Green, 1907; and Salem, NH: Ayer, 1975.

News About the Guild, Being the Magazine of the Guild of the Daughters of Ceres. (From 1909 until 1945, this quarterly journal reported activities at Studley College. Copies are now housed in the University of Reading Library, England.)

Ornstein, Robert E. *The Psychology of Consciousness*. New York: Viking Penguin, 1975.

Regardie, Israel. *The Complete Golden Dawn System*. Phoenix, AZ: New Falcon, 1984.

———. *The Eye in the Triangle*. Phoenix, AZ: New Falcon, 1989.

———. *The Golden Dawn*. St. Paul, MN: Llewellyn, 1986.

Richardson, Alan, ed. *Dancers to the Gods, the Magical records of Charles Seymour and Christine Hartley*. London: Aquarian Press, 1985. Now published in the United States of America by Llewellyn as *Twentieth Century Magic and the Old Religion: Dion Fortune, Christine Hartley, Charles Seymour*.

———. *Priestess*. London: Aquarian Press, 1987.

Summers, Montague. *The Geography of Witchcraft*. New York: Routledge, 1978.

———. *Materials Toward the History of Witchcraft*, 3 Vols. Henry C. Lea and George L. Burr, eds. New York: AMS Pr. Reprint of 1939 edition.

———. *The Vampire: His Kith and Kin*. E. P. Dutton, 1929.

———. *The Werewolf*. New York: Carol Publishing Group, 1973.

Symonds, John. *The Great Beast*. London: Rider, 1951.

———. *The King of the Shadow Realm*. London: Duckworth, 1989.

Symonds, John and Kenneth Grant, editors. *The Confessions of Aleister Crowley*. London: Arkana, 1989.

Torrens, R. G. *The Inner Teachings of the Golden Dawn*. Saffron Walden, England: Neville Spearman, 1969.

Trevelyan, G. M. *A Shortened History of England*. New York: Viking Penguin, 1988.

Waite, A. E. *Shadows of Life and Thought*. Selwyn & Blount, 1938.

Warwick, Frances Evelyn. *Life's Ebb and Flow*. New York: William Morrow, 1929.

———. *Progress in Women's Education in the British Empire*. London: Longmans Green, 1898.

Webb, James. *The Age of the Irrational*. Vol. 1 of *The Flight from Reason*. London: MacDonald, 1971.

Wilson, Colin. *Aleister Crowley: The Nature of the Beast*. London: Aquarian Press, 1988.

————. *The Occult*. New York: Random House, 1973.

Information on mental illness was summarized from pamphlets published by:

National Institute of Mental Health
Public Inquiries, Room 1 5C-105
5600 Fishers Lane
Rockville, MD 20857

and

American Psychiatric Association
1400 K Street NW
Washington, DC 20005

Information on menopause from a pamphlet, "The Menopause Time of Life," published in 1986 by:

National Institute on Aging
2209 Distribution Circle
Silver Springs, MD 20910

Janine Chapman has a B. A. in French, a Master degree in Library Science, and a Master of Science degree in Foreign Language Education from Florida State University. She has taught language to students in grades 4 through 12, and has worked as a librarian. She studied esoteric subjects under many teachers, including Ophiel and W. E. Butler. Chapman lives in Tallahassee, Florida and teaches classes in Qabalah under the aegis of "Mystic Systems," a mystery school she founded. The school is dedicated to a life in harmony with the natural laws of the universe and respect for all spiritual paths.

This photograph was taken when the author was doing this research. She is standing in front of a painting titled "Digital Corn," an acrylic on Plexiglas by J. Michael James.